MEDICINE:
YESTERDAY, TODAY, AND TOMORROW

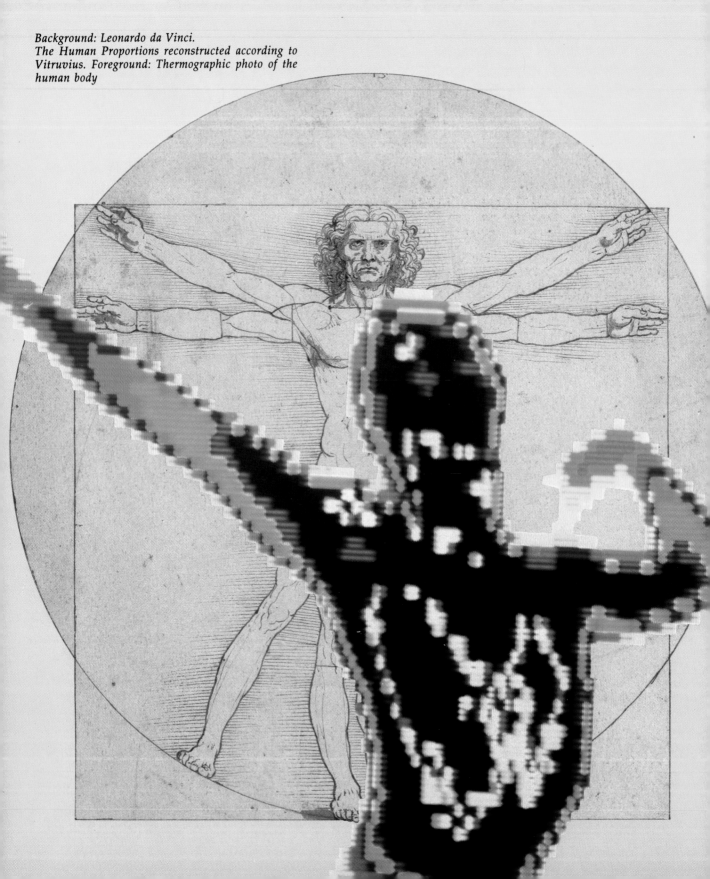

MEDICINE:
YESTERDAY, TODAY, AND TOMORROW

Dennis Brindell Fradin

Consultant:
Robert S. Katz, M.D.
Rush-Presbyterian-St. Luke's Medical Center
Chicago, Illinois

Genetic Engineering Consultant:
Virginia V. Michels, M.D.
Mayo Clinic
Rochester, Minnesota

 CHILDRENS PRESS®
CHICAGO

For My Dear Uncle, Harold Brindell,

With Love

LIBRARY OF CONGRESS
Library of Congress Cataloging-in-Publication Data

Fradin, Dennis B.
   Medicine—yesterday, today, and tomorrow / by Dennis B. Fradin.
     p. cm.
   Includes index.
   Summary: Surveys the history and current status of the field
of medicine and makes future projections about such developments
as genetic engineering and the conquest of disease.
   ISBN 0-516-00538-3
   1. Medicine—Juvenile literature.   [1. Medicine.]   I. Title.
R130.5.F73 1988
610—dc19   88-15336
                                        CIP
                                        AC

Acknowledgments

The author wishes to thank the following individuals and institutions for their help:

Mayo Clinic
Dr. G. David Ball
Dr. Edmund Y. S. Chao
Dr. David N. Fass
Dr. Gerald Gilchrist
Bruce Kall
Dr. Virginia V. Michels
Dr. Charles G. Moertel
Nancy A. Skaran
Dr. Thomas C. Spelsberg
Dr. Sylvester Sterioff

Institute of Gerontology,
University of Michigan
Dr. Richard C. Adelman
Dorothy H. Coons
Dr. Ari Gafni
Dr. Jersey Liang

New York University Medical
Center
Dr. Ruth Nussenzweig
Dr. Roy E. Shore

University of California–
San Francisco
Beverley Atherton
Dr. Edwin C. Cadman
Dr. Kanu Chatterjee
Dr. John W. Danforth
Dr. Oscar Salvatierra Jr.
Robert Sanders

Johns Hopkins Hospital
Dr. A. Michael Borkon
Dr. Jonathan M. Links
Dr. Donald Lowell Price
Dr. Michael X. Repka

United States Centers for
Disease Control
Nancy Arden
Dr. Alan Greenberg
Dr. Marguerite Pappaioanou

Humana Heart Institute
of Louisville, Kentucky
Dr. Richard D. Allen
Dr. Roland E. Girardet
Dr. Allan M. Lansing
Melissa Williams

Evanston Hospital of
Evanston, Illinois
Dr. Hartley S. Begoun
Dr. Deborah V. Edidin

University of Chicago
Dr. Daniel A. Albert
Dr. William Benjamin Gill Jr.

Argonne National Laboratory
Dr. Norman G. Anderson
Dr. Thomas E. Fritz

Harold Brindell
Milton Colman
Thelma Feinstein
Dr. Richard H. Grimm Jr., University of Minnesota
Dr. David E. Harrison, The Jackson Laboratory, Bar Harbor, Maine
Dr. Robert S. Katz, Rush-Presbyterian-St. Luke's Medical Center, Chicago
Marsha Newman, R.Ph.
Dr. Timothy A. Sanborn, Boston University School of Medicine
Kristina Schellinski, UNICEF
Dr. Karl T. Weber, Michael Reese Hospital and Medical Center, Chicago
Dr. Kathryn J. Zerbe, the Menninger Clinic of Topeka, Kansas

CONTENTS

Part I: Yesterday

Part II: Today

Part III: Tomorrow

Part IV: Appendix

Sixteenth-century engraving of a brain operation performed without the aid of anesthesia

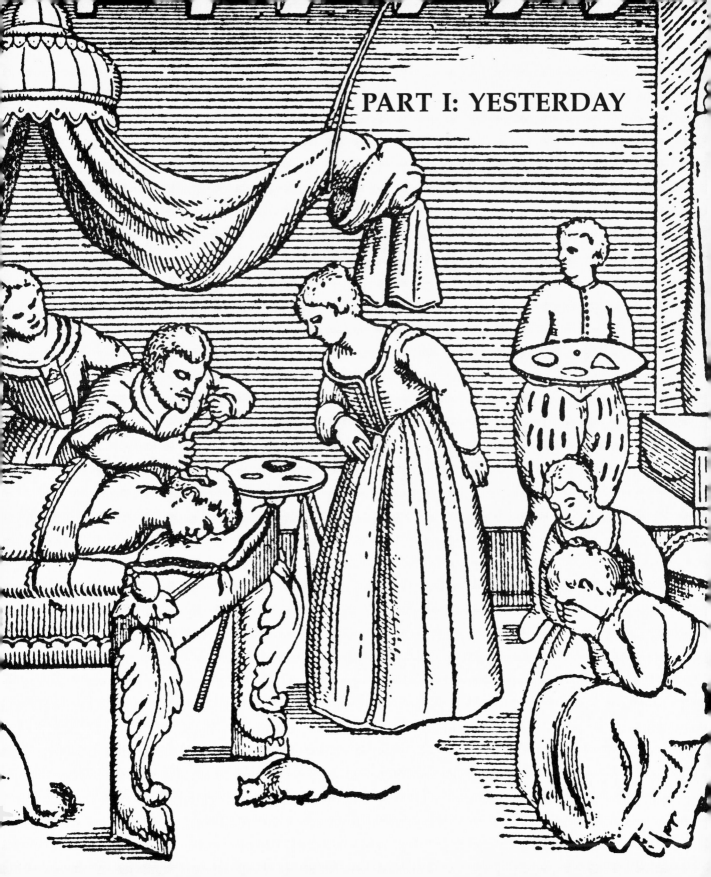

PART I: YESTERDAY

Chapter 1
Ancient Medicine

I will follow that method of treatment which, according to my ability and judgment, I consider for the benefit of my patients. . . . With purity and with holiness I will pass my life and practice my art. . . . Into whatever houses I enter I will go into them for the benefit of the sick. . . .

Oath of Hippocrates, dating from about 400 B.C.

As recently as 1750, people in many countries lived an average of only about thirty years. This was little longer than the average for ancient Greece and Rome. Today, the average life span in many countries is about seventy-five years. The longer, healthier lives enjoyed by many people today are due to advances in medicine—the science of preventing, curing, and treating diseases and injuries.

The life span has soared since 1750 because most of the major medical breakthroughs in history have occurred since then. The first vaccine to prevent disease was not created until 1796. Anesthetics to prevent pain during surgery were not developed until the 1840s. Not until the 1870s were germs proved to cause disease. Surgeons could not do much operating on such delicate organs as the heart and the brain until the mid-1900s.

Why did it take until so recently for these breakthroughs to be made? The major reason was that a vast amount of knowledge had to be gathered first. For example, microscopes had to be invented before germs could be shown to cause disease; and before microscopes could be invented, people had to learn how to make lenses. The properties of various chemicals had to be discovered before anesthetics could be created. And before surgeons could operate on the brain and heart, much had to be learned about those organs. The explosion in medical knowledge that began about 200 years ago (and is still occurring) depended on the work of thousands of earlier people, some dating back to ancient times.

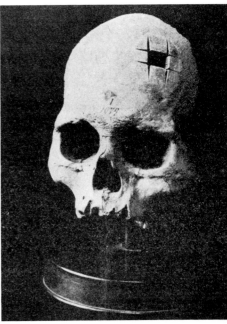

Many of the sources of today's medicines and procedures can be traced to prehistoric times. Cave dwellers (left) used simple methods of healing wounds. Others, such as the Inca of Peru, had knowledge of advanced techniques. Right: Remains of a human skull that was operated on more than 500 years ago

Prehistoric Medicine

The years before people made written records are called prehistoric times. Studies of fossils, which are remains of animals and plants preserved in rock layers in the Earth's crust, reveal that prehistoric people suffered from some of the same diseases as we do. One of the oldest specimens of disease in a human being has been found in the thighbone of a person who lived in Java more than a million years ago. Analysis of the bone revealed that its owner suffered from a tumor.

The oldest fossils showing attempted medical treatment are some skulls found in France, Russia, Spain, Peru, and several other places. In a process called *trephination*, flint knives were used to cut holes in the skulls of living people. Why were these painful operations performed? Probably prehistoric people thought that certain diseases were caused by demons—or evil spirits—trapped inside people's heads. By cutting holes through the patients' skulls, prehistoric surgeons probably thought they were creating a way for the demons to escape.

11

Medicine in Ancient China

Ancient China, one of the birthplaces of civilization, also made quite a few contributions to the development of medicine. The ancient Chinese believed (and many still believe) that two forces, *Yin* and *Yang*, flow through everything in the universe, including the human body. The Chinese thought that when these two forces were out of balance in the body, disease resulted. To restore the proper balance, the ancient Chinese practiced acupuncture, which involves sticking needles into different parts of the body.

Acupuncture is still practiced by millions of the world's people, many of whom claim that their arthritis, migraine headaches, ulcers, and asthma have been cured by it. In recent years, doctors in China have even used acupuncture to kill pain during major surgery. Yet although more than five thousand years have gone by since the Chinese first introduced acupuncture, scientists still do not know how it works.

The ancient Chinese also learned a great deal about drugs. Emperor Shen Nung, who is often called China's first physician, studied drugs in great detail about five thousand years ago. His findings were written down in a book called *Pen Tsao* or *Great Herbal*, which has been reprinted many times right up to the twentieth century. Among the drugs prescribed by Shen Nung that are still in use is ephedrine, a hay fever and asthma medication.

The medical knowledge gathered by the ancient Chinese was placed in a forty-volume encyclopedia entitled *The Golden Mirrors of Medicine*. One example of the advanced nature of this knowledge involves blood circulation. Although the Englishman William Harvey (1578–1657) is usually credited with discovering that blood circulates through the body, the Chinese understood the basics of blood circulation more than four thousand years before Harvey's birth! In *Nei Ching* (*The Book of Medicine*), Emperor Huang-ti wrote: "All the blood in the body is under the control of the heart . . . the blood current flows continuously in a circle, and never stops."

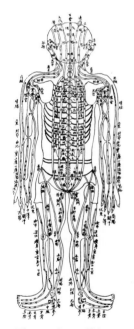

The ancient Chinese acupuncture chart (above) shows the various points on the body where needles can be inserted.

Medicine in Ancient Egypt

Ancient Egypt also played a major role in turning medicine into a science. The Egyptians devised a method of wrapping dead bodies in cloth, called mummification, to preserve them for long periods of time. Through their work with mummies, the Egyptians learned much about the human body. They used this knowledge to devise numerous treatments for diseases and injuries.

Thanks to their mummy-wrapping work, the ancient Egyptians became experts at bandaging wounds. They also treated certain wounds by stitching them or even placing moldy bread on them. What is interesting about the moldy bread treatment is that more than four thousand years later antibiotics extracted from molds were found to kill germs. The Egyptians also knew how to set broken bones, soothe burns, produce drugs from natural substances, and operate on certain tumors.

The Egyptians produced one of the first known physicians— Imhotep—who was so revered that after his death he was worshiped as a god and temples were built in his honor. The ancient Egyptians also had female physicians. Later, unfortunately, women were generally excluded from practicing medicine.

An Egyptian physician (bottom left) treats a patient with lockjaw. Right: The Egyptian physician Imhotep

Medicine in Ancient Israel

The people of ancient times knew nothing about germs. Yet experience taught them that certain conditions seemed to bring on disease. The ancient Jewish people created a complex system of health laws based on their experiences.

The Jews divided foods into kosher foods, which they could eat, and nonkosher foods, which were forbidden. Pork (meat from hogs) is a well-known nonkosher food. One reason pork was forbidden was that in those days it often contained tapeworms and trichina worms, both of which can cause illness in humans. The Jews did not know why the meat caused illness; but after observing what happened to many people after eating pork, they banned it.

The Jews were also among the first to devise methods for preventing epidemics—large-scale outbreaks of disease. They separated sick people from the rest of the community and thoroughly cleaned their property. The Jews did not know that infected people could pass germs on to others, but experience taught them that one sick person could somehow infect an entire community.

Medicine in Ancient India

Ancient India made a vital contribution to medicine by helping to make surgery into a science. By about 700 B.C. Indian doctors were performing many operations. They were among the first to deliver babies by cesarean section. This method, which is sometimes necessary to save the lives of mother and child, involves delivering the baby through an incision in the mother's abdomen and uterus rather than through her birth canal. Indian doctors were also among the first to do plastic surgery—the repair of injured, defective, or misshapen body parts using transplanted healthy tissue.

In addition, the people of ancient India discovered the immediate causes of several kinds of epidemics. They observed that bubonic plague strikes when rats are present and that malaria is spread by mosquitoes. They did not know that fleas on the rats had germs that

Evidence that plastic surgery was practiced in India more than 2,000 years ago has been found in ancient Indian texts.

cause bubonic plague, nor did they understand that germs carried by the mosquitoes cause malaria. However, by identifying the animals that carried those germs, they took the first steps toward controlling plague and malaria.

Medicine in Ancient Greece

More than twenty-five hundred years ago, the people of Greece created a civilization so important that its influence is felt strongly even today. The Greeks excelled at mathematics, philosophy, drama, poetry, sports, architecture, sculpture, music, and the sciences, including medicine.

The Greeks believed that their god of healing, Asclepius, had the power to revive the dead. Starting around 700 B.C. they built many temples to honor Asclepius and brought the sick there to be healed.

The patients in the temples spent a great deal of time sleeping so that Asclepius could appear to them in their dreams. The temple priests prescribed medical treatments based on what Asclepius said or did in the dreams. The temples also had physicians who placed the patients on special diets, bathed them in hot spring water, and

Below: The Greek Temple of Asclepius

gave them medicines, massages, and exercise. With the passing of centuries Greek medicine became more scientific. The priests' role in treating the sick diminished while that of the doctors increased.

From about 461 B.C. until the early 400s B.C. Greece enjoyed its "Golden Age." Among the famous people who lived during the Golden Age were the philosopher Socrates; the playwrights Aeschylus, Sophocles, and Euripides; the historian Herodotus; and the most famous doctor of all time, Hippocrates.

Born in about 460 B.C. on the Greek island of Kos, Hippocrates received his early medical training from his physician father. After becoming a doctor himself, Hippocrates practiced medicine on his home island and in various other places, including Athens, which was then the world's most important city. Hippocrates brought a new outlook to medicine—a totally scientific one. Magic and superstition had no place in medicine in Hippocrates' view. He said that diseases had natural causes that doctors must understand in order to provide patients with the best possible care.

Hippocrates believed that "the healing power of Nature" was as

Hippocrates

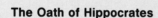

The Oath of Hippocrates

I swear by Apollo, the physician, and Asclepius and Health and All-Heal and all the gods and goddesses that, according to my ability and judgment, I will keep this oath and stipulation:

To reckon him who taught me this art equally dear to me as my parents, to share my substance with him and relieve his necessities if required; to regard his offspring as on the same footing with my own brothers, and to teach them this art if they should wish to learn it, without fee or stipulation, and that by precept, lecture, and every other mode of instruction, I will impart a knowledge of the art to my own sons and to those of my teachers, and to disciples bound by a stipulation and oath, according to the law of medicine, but to none others.

I will follow that method of treatment which, according to my ability and judgment, I consider for the benefit of my patients, and abstain from whatever is deleterious and mischievous. I will give no deadly medicine to anyone if asked, nor suggest any such counsel; furthermore, I will not give to a woman an instrument to produce abortion.

With purity and with holiness I will pass my life and practice my art. I will not cut a person who is suffering from a stone, but will leave this to be done by practitioners of this work. Into whatever houses I enter I will go into them for the benefit of the sick and will abstain from every voluntary act of mischief and corruption; and further from the seduction of females or males, bond or free.

Whatever, in connection with my professional practice, or not in connection with it, I may see or hear in the lives of men which ought not to be spoken abroad I will not divulge, as reckoning that all such should be kept secret.

While I continue to keep this oath unviolated may it be granted to me to enjoy life and the practice of the art, respected by all men at all times but should I trespass and violate this oath, may the reverse be my lot.

important as the doctor in helping the sick. His favorite prescriptions were water and honey for thirst and vinegar and honey for pain, and he only resorted to strong drugs when absolutely necessary. He performed various kinds of surgery, but only after all other treatments had failed. Hippocrates also understood that good diet, fresh air, and rest are necessary for the recovery of sick persons.

Hippocrates' observations are contained in the "Hippocratic Collection," consisting of about a hundred books. Although most of these books were probably written by Hippocrates' followers, they are thought to contain his basic beliefs. The best-known selection from these works is Hippocrates' famous oath, which is still recited by many graduating students of medicine. Also famous are the aphorisms (sayings) of Hippocrates, which include these:

> When sleep puts an end to delirium it is a good sign.
>
> All diseases occur at all seasons, but some diseases are more apt to occur and to be aggravated at certain seasons.
>
> In winter occur pleurisy, pneumonia, colds, sore throats, headaches, dizziness, apoplexy [strokes].
>
> If there be a painful affection in any part of the body, and yet no suffering, there is mental disorder.
>
> The old have fewer illnesses than the young, but if any become chronic with them they generally carry it with them to the grave.
>
> Those naturally very fat are more liable to sudden death than the thin.
>
> Do not disturb a patient either during or just after a crisis....
>
> Weariness without [apparent] cause indicates disease.
>
> When one oversleeps, or fails to sleep, the condition suggests disease.

Because he popularized the idea that medicine must be scientific, Hippocrates is called the "Father of Modern Medicine." However, so that we do not paint too rosy a picture of medicine during Greece's "Golden Age," several facts must be added. Hippocrates and his fellow doctors often had to trust in "the healing power of Nature" because they themselves lacked the ability to cure many diseases. For example, when bubonic plague struck Athens in 430 B.C., doctors could only watch helplessly as nearly a third of the city's people died. It also must be mentioned that in ancient Greece and in most other places up until recent times, only the wealthy received good medical care. The steady improvements in medicine made little difference to the poorer people.

Roman Medical Advances

By 146 B.C. Greece had been conquered by the Romans, who were building one of the most powerful empires in history. The Romans gained much of their medical knowledge from Greece and from Egypt, another of their conquered lands. They also made several contributions of their own.

Although nothing was yet known about germs, the Romans observed that sewage and dirty drinking water caused epidemics. To bring clean water to Rome they built fourteen aqueducts, which carried three hundred million gallons of fresh drinking water to the city every day. They also built an extensive sewerage system to remove wastes from Rome's streets. Parts of the Roman sewerage system are still used, more than two thousand years later.

The Romans also built some of the first hospitals. The purpose of the earliest ones was to provide first aid to injured soldiers, but later hospitals met the needs of the general public. Our word *hospital* comes from Latin, the language of the Romans. It originated from the Latin word *hospitalis*, meaning "house for guests."

The Roman Empire also produced a doctor who for a long time influenced medicine even more strongly than did Hippocrates. His name was Galen, and he was born in present-day Turkey in about A.D. 130. One of Galen's great interests was anatomy—the structure of living things. He learned much about human anatomy by serving

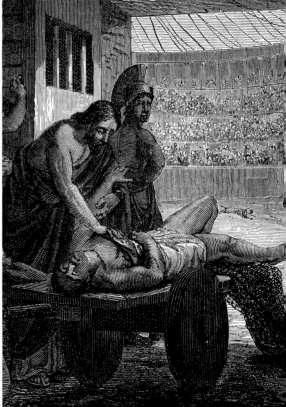

Galen was both a surgeon (right) and a pharmacist (left). His formulas for preparing medicines were used in the West for more than 1,000 years.

as a surgeon to gladiators (trained fighters who entertained the Romans) and by studying and practicing medicine in several Roman cities. However, because it was illegal at the time to dissect, or cut apart, dead human bodies, Galen was forced to do much of his anatomical research on monkeys and pigs.

Galen made several important discoveries. He proved that the blood vessels called *arteries* contain blood, not air as many had believed. He also showed that the heart is the organ that pumps blood. For these and other discoveries, Galen is often called the second greatest medical figure of ancient times—after Hippocrates. Unfortunately, Galen's reputation became so great that it hampered future medical progress.

The problem was Galen's belief that human organs were almost exactly like those of the animals he had dissected. Because of this, Galen made many mistakes about human anatomy in the more than four hundred books he wrote. Centuries were to pass before the mistaken ideas of Galen would be challenged successfully.

Chapter 2
The Middle Ages

```
A B R A C A D A B R A
 A B R A C A D A B R
  A B R A C A D A B
   A B R A C A D A
    A B R A C A D
     A B R A C A
      A B R A C
       A B R A
        A B R
         A B
          A
```

Magic charm the sick wore around their necks during the Middle Ages

The Europeans

The term *Middle Ages* is used to describe the period in European history from about A.D. 400 to about A.D. 1400. During this time few additions were made to humanity's general knowledge. In fact, so much of the knowledge gathered over the centuries by the Greeks and Romans was lost during the Middle Ages that these years are often called the *Dark Ages*. Scattered monasteries and schools were among the few places where learning flourished.

The Middle Ages were especially dark when it came to people's health. The Roman system of bringing fresh water into a city and getting rid of sewage was forgotten. People in the overcrowded cit-

ies tossed their garbage right onto the streets, and water was allowed to sit in stinking pools. Because of this, rats and other disease-causing organisms that thrived on garbage and stale water became widespread pests. The result was a string of epidemics so terrible that many people still think of plagues and disease whenever the Middle Ages are mentioned.

Between the years 500 and 650 numerous bubonic plague epidemics killed about 100 million people in Europe and Asia. However, the single worst bubonic plague epidemic—and probably the worst disaster *ever* to strike human beings—was the plague that ravaged Europe and Asia between 1330 and 1350. Known as the *Black Death*, this massive epidemic killed about 75 million people, or about one-fourth of the world's population, in twenty years. At times, it appeared that the Black Death might put an end to the entire human species.

The Black Death would not have occurred had people realized that bubonic plague was transmitted by fleas on rats, and that by keeping cities clean people could limit the rat population. The people of ancient India had understood the rat-plague connection, but during the Middle Ages few people thought about the scientific causes of things. Instead they blamed their troubles on demons, on mysterious vapors in the air, or on unlucky alignments of the heavenly bodies. For example, it was widely thought that the Black Death was caused by an unlucky positioning of the planets Mars, Jupiter, and Saturn in the sky.

Below: The plague of 1656 in Rome

The belief that star and planet positions control our destinies is a false science called astrology. Today it would be difficult to find any scientists who believe in astrology, but most of the people of the Middle Ages believed in it. The wealthy hired astrologers to determine the luckiest times for going on trips, making business deals, or receiving medical care.

Very little medical care was available in Europe during the Middle Ages. Doctors did little examining of patients to diagnose disease. Instead, many asked patients their symptoms and then tried to determine what was wrong based on what they said. Some doctors bragged that they could diagnose what was wrong just by looking at the patient's urine. For example, if the top layer of the urine was murky, this meant that the patient had a disease of the head!

Treatment was just as unscientific. The ancient practice of drilling holes in the skull to treat a variety of head problems was again in vogue. Also popular was *bloodletting* or "bleeding." This involved drawing out a portion of the patient's blood either by cutting veins or by attaching blood-sucking worms called *leeches* to the body. The thought of this may make us squirm, but the doctors of the Middle Ages were convinced that bloodletting allowed diseases to exit the body in the blood. Although many patients weakened and died from bloodletting, the practice was popular well into the 1800s.

The doctors of the Middle Ages used a variety of medicines, few of which had any value. There was a widespread belief that medicines had to be disgusting enough to drive off disease. As a result, doctors did their best to think up vile medicines for people to eat, bathe in, or drink. Among the popular substances were human and animal urine and excrement; powder from Egyptian mummies; animal hooves; and various parts of snakes, frogs, and lizards.

Foul smells supposedly could drive off the mysterious vapors in the air that were thought to cause some diseases. One farfetched scheme for driving away the Black Death involved keeping dirty goats inside the house. Another involved having people expel gas into jars, which were saved and then opened when the Black Death was in the neighborhood!

The above drawings depict common medical practices of the Middle Ages: bleeding the patients (left) and drilling holes in their skulls (right).

Many people also believed that, as the Christian leader Saint Augustine (A.D. 354–430) said, "All diseases are to be ascribed to Demons." Magical words and relics of saints were thought to have the power to drive away these demons. Besides the "medicines" they prescribed, many doctors gave their patients charms containing a few Latin words to wear around their necks, and saints' bones or pieces of saints' clothing to hold in their hands.

The medical care described above was available mainly to wealthy Europeans. The poor people of Europe rarely received any kind of medical care at all during the Middle Ages.

The main reason for the lack of medical progress during these centuries was that experimentation was nearly dead. When doctors today want to learn more about the human body they dissect cadavers (dead bodies). During the Middle Ages, the cutting apart of human bodies was for the most part banned by religious leaders. Doctors also lacked the curiosity that today is considered an important characteristic of a good scientist. Most doctors were repulsed by the idea of touching dead bodies and were content to read what Galen, the ancient Roman surgeon, had written to settle a medical question. The result was that the same medical mistakes were repeated over and over for a thousand years.

A few medical advances were made during the Middle Ages. The two main European contributions were the building of medical schools and the founding of new hospitals. One of the first European medical schools was founded at Salerno, Italy, during the 800s. Be-

In France The Great Room of the Poor (La Grand Chambre des Pauvres) *is believed to be the oldest hospital in continuous use throughout five hundred years.*

fore the founding of this school, one could become a doctor just by studying for a time with another doctor. The Medical School of Salerno required its students to pass certain courses and meet certain standards before they could become doctors. Other European medical schools founded during the Middle Ages included ones at Bologna and Padua in Italy and Montpellier in France.

During the Middle Ages hospitals were built in many cities to care for orphans, the aged, the blind, and the sick. But these hospitals were generally dirty, overcrowded places where doctors and nurses could do little more than comfort patients before they died.

The Muslims

As Europeans wallowed in ignorance during the Middle Ages, the Muslims (followers of the religion Islam) were making progress in many fields, including medicine. The Muslims, who controlled much of Asia, translated ancient Greek medical texts, thus helping to preserve the knowledge gathered by the ancients. Among their original contributions were the founding of higher-quality hospitals than those in Europe. By 1000 every Muslim city had its own hospital. Baghdad, in what is now Iraq, had sixty hospitals.

Many of the Islamic doctors were better educated than their Euro-

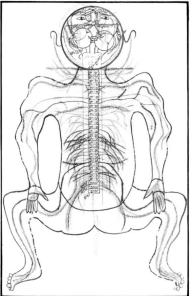
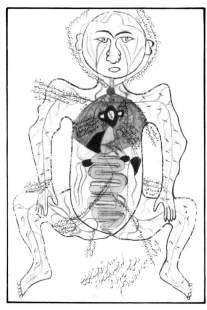

pean counterparts. The most famous of the Islamic doctors was Ibn-Sina, who is usually known as Avicenna (980–1037). Born in present-day Russia, Avicenna memorized the Muslims' sacred book, the *Koran*, by age ten. At eighteen he was made court physician to a king, who allowed him to use the royal library. Avicenna read so much that by twenty he was considered the world's foremost scholar. Besides becoming a well-known poet and astronomer, Avicenna gained fame as one of the most brilliant physicians of his day.

Rather than merely trusting in the books he had read, Avicenna did much original research on diagnosing and treating diseases. He wrote numerous medical books, including the *Canon of Medicine*, often called the most influential medical textbook of all time. The *Canon* was used as a text in Asia and Europe for more than six centuries, and is sometimes consulted by Asian doctors even today.

However, like almost all the other doctors of his time, Avicenna had some bizarre ideas for curing diseases. For example, he said that lice should be inserted into the urinary tracts of people who had trouble urinating. The idea was that the lice would suck out the urine! Suggested by one of the greatest doctors since Hippocrates, this unusual treatment demonstrates how ignorant even the best physicians of the Middle Ages were about medical matters.

Far left: Avicenna, Islamic physician. Above: Ancient Arabic drawings of the human anatomy

Chapter 3
The Renaissance

It is not title and eloquence, nor the knowledge of the language, nor the reading of books, however ornamental, that are the requirements of a physician, but the deepest knowledge of things themselves and of nature's secrets and this knowledge outweighs all else. . . .

Paracelsus (physician who
lived from about 1493 to 1541)

By the year 1400 the human mind that had for the most part been asleep for ten centuries began to stir. The period of renewed interest in learning that occurred in Europe between the years 1400 and 1600 is called the *Renaissance*, a French word meaning "rebirth."

There were several reasons for this renewed interest in learning. For one thing, during the late Middle Ages Europeans had come into contact with the Islamic Arabs, who had preserved many ancient manuscripts and had also made many scientific discoveries of their own. The Arabs' interest in learning inspired the Europeans. The invention of printing also contributed to the Renaissance.

Until the mid-1400s the only way to produce a book was to copy it by hand. Think how long it would take you to copy this book, which has about fifty thousand words in it. Now imagine how long it must have taken to make one copy of Avicenna's *Canon of Medicine*, which had about a million words. Because it took so long to copy them by hand, books were very expensive and scarce.

In about 1440 the German printer Johannes Gutenberg invented movable type, which allowed printers to produce hundreds of copies of a book in a day, as opposed to one copy in hundreds of days. By the year 1500 more than a thousand printing shops were operating throughout Europe. People who formerly had been unable to afford books could now obtain the works of the ancients that were being reprinted as well as books by new authors.

In science one thinker inspires another. All the books that were suddenly available inspired Renaissance thinkers to do research. For example, Nicolaus Copernicus (1473–1543) of Poland and other astronomers read about the theories of the ancient stargazers and questioned their accuracy. To learn the truth, they began to study the night sky carefully. In doing so, they shaped astronomy into a modern science. Similarly, a number of great thinkers led medicine out of the Dark Ages.

A prime reason that progress in medicine had stood still for over a thousand years was that doctors had spent little time studying human anatomy. Renaissance scientists realized that the only way to find out if the ancients had been right about the body was to dissect cadavers. One of the most important persons to do this was Leonardo da Vinci (1452–1519).

Born near the Italian city of Florence, Leonardo became famous for his paintings, which included the *Mona Lisa* and *The Last Supper*. He was also an amateur scientist who made numerous discoveries in the fields of astronomy, biology, and medicine. Partly because he wanted to portray the human body accurately in his artwork, Leonardo dissected cadavers and made hundreds of drawings to record his findings. By the time religious officials stopped him from cutting up bodies, Leonardo had learned that Galen, hailed as *the* anatomy expert for thirteen centuries, had made many errors.

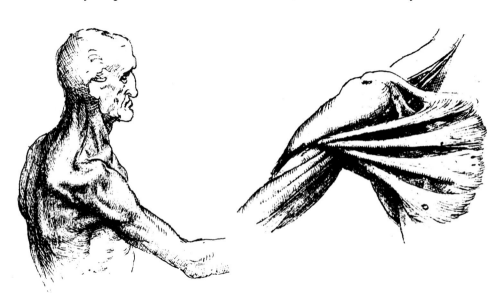

Study of the muscles of the shoulder, neck, and arm by Leonardo da Vinci, 1510

Leonardo set the tone for a new age in medicine when he wrote that scientists should not depend totally on old authors but should "rely on experience." He added that "those who study only old authors and not the works of nature are stepsons, not sons of Nature."

As more and more doctors wanted to learn firsthand about the human body, religious leaders relaxed the ban on dissection. By the mid-1500s dissection of cadavers was becoming popular in medical schools. The greatest anatomist of the Renaissance, Andreas Vesalius (1514–1564), was at work by then.

Vesalius was born in Brussels, Belgium, five years before the death of Leonardo. As a schoolboy, Vesalius dissected cats, dogs, and mice. While studying medicine in Louvain, Belgium, where human dissection was still outlawed, Vesalius helped steal the body of a hanged criminal and then took part in dissecting it. Later he went to study anatomy at Padua, Italy, where doctors could dissect bodies without having to steal them.

Below: Engraving of Andreas Vesalius. Right: Vesalius's chart of the human nervous system

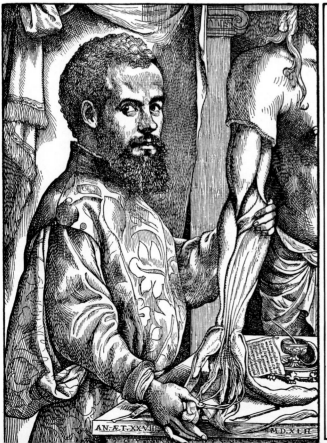

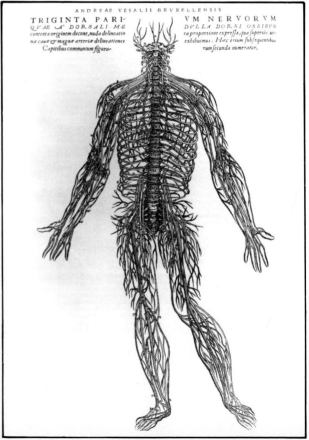

Vesalius became so knowledgeable about the human body that at age twenty-three he was made Professor of Anatomy at the University of Padua. In 1543 Vesalius published his anatomical findings in *De humani corporis fabrica* (*Concerning the fabric of the human body*). This book, which revealed so much about the body, came out less than a week after the publication of Copernicus's *De revolutionibus orbium coelestium* (*On the revolutions of the celestial spheres*), which revealed so much about the universe's true nature.

Today Vesalius is called the "Father of Anatomy" and *De humani corporis fabrica* is hailed as one of the most important books in the history of science. However, in his own day Vesalius was ridiculed by those who supported Galen. Vesalius was so upset by all the criticism that he burned his writings and left the University of Padua shortly after the book was published. Nevertheless, Vesalius's work inspired others to continue studying the human body.

Theophrastus Bombastus von Hohenheim (1493?–1541), known as Paracelsus, was another great Renaissance physician who suffered ridicule. The son of a doctor, Paracelsus was born in Switzerland. He studied in Austria and Italy and practiced medicine in Spain, Portugal, Italy, France, Germany, Switzerland, Sweden, Russia, Poland, Turkey, and present-day Yugoslavia. As he journeyed, Paracelsus wrote books, lectured, and treated patients with remarkable success.

Paracelsus

However, overshadowing Paracelsus's medical successes were his opinions, which got him kicked out of many towns. For example, after Paracelsus became a professor at Basel University in Switzerland in 1527 he annoyed his colleagues by publicly burning the books of Galen and Avicenna. "This is the cause of the misery of this world," he told his fellow doctors, "that your science is founded upon lies. You are not professors of the truth, but professors of falsehood." Such statements earned Paracelsus the hatred of many of his fellow doctors. However, the admiration of his patients must have consoled the man who said that "a physician should exercise his art not for his own benefit but for the sake of his patient."

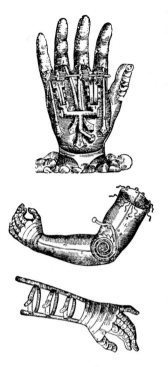

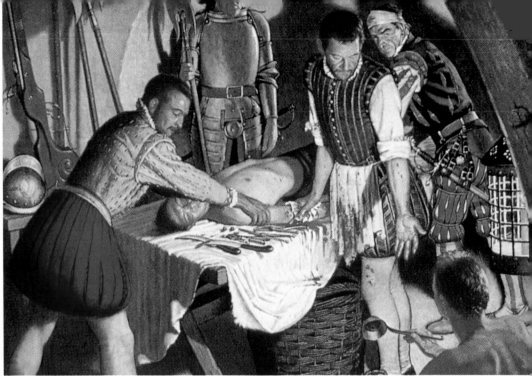

Ambroise Paré (right) treating a wound with boiling oil. Above: His drawings of artificial limbs

While Vesalius was becoming the "Father of Anatomy" and Paracelsus was making his mark as the medical profession's conscience, Ambroise Paré (1510?–1590) was earning a reputation as the "Father of Modern Surgery." Born near Laval, France, Paré grew up in a family of barber-surgeons. The idea of barbers performing surgery seems strange today, but in those days doctors generally refused to do surgery (partly because most operations ended in failure). This often left barbers as the only ones with the tools and the desire to operate.

Paré studied the family business, but soon found that he liked the surgery part better than cutting hair. After sharpening his surgical skills at a Paris hospital, Paré became an army surgeon—a job he held for thirty years. While working on the battlefield, Paré discovered many principles that still govern surgery.

In Paré's time doctors poured boiling oil on gunshot and other wounds to drive out what they thought was the poison in the injuries. Paré used this painful procedure until the day he ran out of oil on the battlefield. Following his instincts, Paré placed a soothing ointment on his patients' wounds. In *Apology and Treatise containing the Voyages Made in Diverse Places*, Paré described how he couldn't sleep for fear that the patients treated with the ointment wouldn't do as well as those he had treated with the boiling oil. When he went out early the next morning to check his patients, however, this is what he saw:

> . . . *beyond my expectation, I found that they to whom I had applied my ointment had suffered but little pain and their wounds [were] without inflammation or swelling. . . . The others, to whom the boiling oil was applied, I found feverish, with great pain, and swelling round the edges of their wounds. Then I resolved never more to cruelly burn these poor men with gunshot wounds.*

Paré made many other surgical discoveries. He learned that the best way to stop bleeding after an amputation was to stitch up the wound. He designed a forceps to grasp arteries and developed other surgical instruments as well as artificial hands and arms. The "Father of Modern Surgery," who operated a private practice when his days as an army surgeon ended, also learned that it was sometimes best to turn the unborn baby within its mother's uterus when the baby was in the wrong position to be born.

Vesalius, Paracelsus, Paré, and a few other dedicated doctors led medicine out of the Dark Ages, but they certainly did not bring it into the sunlight. By the year 1600, which marked the end of the Renaissance, medicine was still quite primitive. Because they knew so little about most diseases, doctors lumped many of them together as "fevers" or "plagues." Bloodletting was still popular, many doctors wouldn't make a move without consulting their astrologers, and many other strange ideas were still popular. For example, Paracelsus recommended placing spotted lizard skins on malignant tumors to cure them. Ambroise Paré, like most other people of the time, believed in witches. Were it not for some dedicated people who led medicine and the other sciences even further out of the darkness, doctors today might still be placing lizard skins on tumors and examining people for odd moles to see if they were witches.

Chapter 4
The Seventeenth and Eighteenth Centuries

*While I was talking to an old man . . . my eye fell upon his
teeth, which were all coated over; so I asked him when he had
last cleaned his mouth. And I got for answer that he'd never
washed his mouth in all his life. So I took some spittle out of
his mouth and . . . also took some of the matter that was
lodged between and against his teeth, and [examining it
under the microscope] . . . I found an unbelievably great com-
pany of living animalcules, a-swimming more nimbly than
any I had ever seen up to this time.*

From a letter written in 1683
by Anton van Leeuwenhoek,
discoverer of bacteria

The Seventeenth Century

The 1600s were a time when scientists learned a great deal about
the workings of many things—from heavenly bodies to human
ones. In 1608 the Dutch optician Hans Lippershey made the first
telescope, and soon after that the great Italian scientist Galileo
(1564–1642) began building telescopes. Galileo used his telescopes
to prove that Copernicus had been right—Earth was not the center
of the Universe but was just a tiny part of it. During the entire seven-
teenth century scientists questioned the ideas of the past and
sought truth by gathering "the deepest knowledge of things themselves," as Paracelsus had advised.

William Harvey (1578–1657) was one of the foremost of these
questioners. Born in Folkestone, England, Harvey studied medicine
in Padua, Italy, and then went to work at St. Bartholomew's Hospital in London. Harvey was very interested in the heart, arteries,
veins, and other parts of the circulatory system. For fourteen years
he dissected the circulatory systems of animals and human beings.

William Harvey demonstrating the circulation of blood to King Charles I and his son

Finally, he concluded that the heart was not an endless fountain of blood, as had been believed. Instead the blood circulated throughout the body. It flowed in a continuous stream through the blood vessels and the heart, repeating that journey again and again.

On April 16, 1616, Harvey explained his findings about blood circulation in a famous lecture. Because he was challenging the long-held viewpoint, Harvey said that "I not only fear injury to myself from the envy of a few, but I tremble lest I have mankind at large for my enemies." Fortunately for Harvey, by this time doctors were more willing to listen to a new theory if it was backed by proof. When Harvey published a book entitled *Exercitatio Anatomica de Motu Cordis et Sanguinis in Animalibus (An Anatomical Treatise on the Motion of the Heart and Blood in Animals)*, most doctors accepted his findings. Some historians say that Harvey did not really discover blood circulation because several ancients had mentioned the theory. Nevertheless, thanks to Harvey's work, the idea of blood circulation became popular.

Anton van Leeuwenhoek was the first to report having seen (what later would be called) protozoa and bacteria.

One reason scientists had trouble learning about the human body was that many structures were too small for the eye to see. Just as telescopes had enabled astronomers to view distant objects, doctors needed an instrument that would reveal very small objects. In 1590 Zacharias Janssen of The Netherlands had invented a microscope that could enlarge small objects, but the problem was that the first microscopes worked poorly. Some of the first microscopes that worked well were made by the great amateur scientist Anton van Leeuwenhoek (1632–1723) of Delft, The Netherlands.

Leeuwenhoek seemed an unlikely prospect to become a great scientist. Poorly educated, he operated a dry goods store in Delft where he enjoyed looking at cloth, coins, and other items with a magnifying glass. Curious as to how these objects would look under higher magnification, Leeuwenhoek began grinding lenses in about 1660 that he used to make the best microscopes of his time.

Still working in his store by day, at night Leeuwenhoek studied bees, houseflies, blood, and many other objects with his microscopes. How different these things appeared when magnified nearly 300 times! Looking at droplets of stagnant water and at some material from his own mouth, Leeuwenhoek saw thousands of what he called "animalcules" and "wretched beasties" swimming

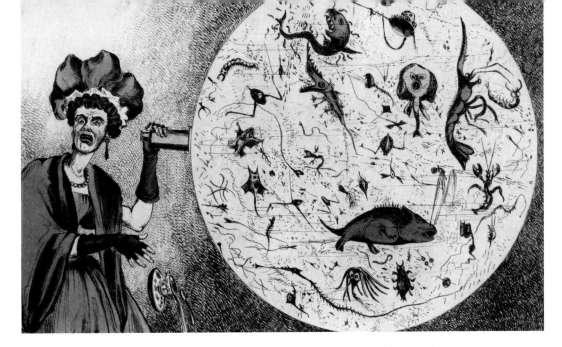

about. Leeuwenhoek had discovered bacteria. He did not know that bacteria cause disease, but his work paved the way for future scientists to make this connection.

Today, doctors depend on the microscope to help them diagnose diseases. For that, we can thank the pioneering work of the Delft storekeeper, Anton van Leeuwenhoek. This great amateur scientist also altered humanity's concept of the universe. Just when people were getting used to the idea that the universe was far larger than had been thought, Leeuwenhoek proved that there were living things in it much smaller than anyone had imagined!

The Eighteenth Century

The years from 1701 to 1800 are often called medicine's "Age of Consolidation." This means that during those years doctors put the knowledge gained in past years into general use. Growing numbers of doctors were studying the human body with the thoroughness of Vesalius, operating using Paré's methods, and practicing with Paracelsus's high standards. There was also a growing respect for medical teaching, as people realized that one great professor could train hundreds of future doctors.

This nineteenth-century etching depicts the horror many people felt after learning that microscopic animals lived in water.

Hermann Boerhaave (above) and some of his patients (right) at the University of Leiden Hospital

Hermann Boerhaave (1668–1738) of Leiden in The Netherlands was one of the greatest of the "consolidators." Although Boerhaave was one of the first to routinely conduct autopsies (examinations of corpses to determine the cause of death or the effects of disease), he made no great discoveries. Yet because of his excellence as a doctor and teacher he is often called the greatest doctor of modern times. Patients came from across Europe to seek Boerhaave's opinion, and students came from far and wide to study with him. Many of Boerhaave's students became the world's best doctors, as did his students' students, and so on.

Some original medical contributions were also made during the eighteenth century. The Scottish surgeon John Hunter (1728–1793) devised a successful operation for aneurysm (weakening of a portion of the wall of a blood vessel, causing the weakened part to balloon outward). In 1785 the English doctor William Withering began treating heart patients with digitalis, a drug (still used today) that is made from the leaves of the purple foxglove flower. However, the greatest breakthrough in the war against disease during the 1700s was the discovery of a way to conquer smallpox.

Because smallpox is no longer a threat, it is difficult for us to imagine the terror that the disease once inspired. Caused by a virus and easily spread from person to person, smallpox was so common that in many countries most of the people caught the disease sometime in their lives. Smallpox victims developed a high fever and a rash that gave the disease its name. During epidemics, one out of every five smallpox patients died, and many of the survivors were

Lady Montagu (above) and John Hunter (left)

blinded by the disease and/or badly scarred by the rash. In the eighteenth century, about sixty million Europeans contracted smallpox. The result was the death, blinding, or disfigurement of one quarter of the continent's population.

The only merciful aspect of smallpox was the fact that people could get it only once. After surviving the first attack, the victim developed immunity (the ability to fight off a particular disease) to further attacks of smallpox. Because of this, parents hoped that their children would get mild cases of smallpox so that they wouldn't have to worry about getting serious cases later in life.

The Englishwoman Lady Mary Wortley Montagu (1689–1762) was one of the first to suggest a way to conquer smallpox. While in Constantinople (now Istanbul, Turkey), Lady Montagu observed the Turks injecting children with fluid from smallpox sores. Those inoculated in this way came down with mild cases of smallpox, but then developed an immunity that protected them from getting serious cases. On April 1, 1717, Lady Montagu wrote a letter to a friend in England about this process:

> *The smallpox, so fatal and general amongst us, is here entirely harmless by the invention of engrafting, which is the name they give it. There is a set of old women who make it their business to perform the operation every autumn in the month of September, when the great heat is abated. People send to one another to know if any of their family has a mind to have the smallpox; they make parties for this purpose and when they are met (commonly fifteen or sixteen together) the old woman comes with a nut-shell of the matter of the best small-*

pox and asks what veins you please to have opened. She imme-diately rips open that [which] you offer her with a large needle (which gives you no more pain than a common scratch) and puts into the vein as much venom as can be upon the head of her needle, and after binds up the little wound with a hol-low bit of shell; and in this way opens four or five veins. . . . The children or young patients play together all the rest of the day, and are in perfect health to the eighth. Then the fever be-gins to seize them, and they keep their beds two days, very sel-dom three. They have very rarely above twenty or thirty [pocks] in their faces, which never mark [scar]; and in eight days' time they are as well as before their illness. . . . I am pa-triot enough to take pain to bring this useful invention into fashion in England; and I should not fail to write to some of our doctors very particularly about it, if I knew any one of them that I thought had virtue enough to destroy such a con-siderable branch of their revenue for the good of mankind.

Thousands of people in England including the children of Lady Montagu and those of the British royal family were inoculated with smallpox. Although this method usually worked, sometimes the pa-tient was given too strong a dose of smallpox and died. Lady Montagu had placed scientists on the right track, but a safer method of preventing smallpox was needed.

The discovery that led to the ultimate conquest of smallpox was made by the Englishman Edward Jenner (1749–1823). Born in Berkeley, England, Jenner was what we would call a "country doc-tor" in that town. In his practice, Jenner learned of a method used by local farmers to avoid smallpox. By touching infected cows, they contracted the mild disease cowpox that was closely related to smallpox. After the bout with cowpox, they were immune to the much more serious disease, smallpox.

For many years Jenner wondered if he could help people avoid smallpox by injecting them with doses of cowpox. Finally, in May of 1796 Jenner learned that a dairymaid named Sarah Nelmes was suffering from cowpox. Deciding that it was time to test his theory, Jenner took some fluid from the girl's arm and on May 14, 1796, he

Edward Jenner

Edward Jenner (center) gives the first smallpox vaccination.

injected it into a boy named James Phipps. Once James recovered from his mild case of cowpox, Dr. Jenner injected him with a strong dose of smallpox.

Twelve days passed—the time it took for smallpox symptoms to appear—and still the eight-year-old boy developed no signs of smallpox. With the help of his farm neighbors who had known of this method for years, Dr. Edward Jenner had made one of the greatest medical discoveries of all time. He had proved that the relatively harmless disease cowpox could be used to immunize people against smallpox.

James Phipps had been given the first vaccination by Dr. Jenner. Vaccines, which are given as shots or by mouth, are preparations that stimulate the body to build up immunity to disease by exposing it to germs that are dead or harmless. Within a few years, vaccination became the standard way of avoiding smallpox. In the years following Jenner, more and more people were vaccinated against smallpox until finally during the late 1970s the smallpox disease was wiped out!

Scientists did not learn how the body develops immunity against disease until a hundred years after Edward Jenner's great discovery. Even though its mechanisms were a mystery, however, the smallpox vaccine worked. Soon other scientists were trying to develop vaccines against many other diseases.

Chapter 5
The Glorious Nineteenth Century

Do not fear to defend new ideas, even the most revolutionary. Your own faith is what counts most. But have courage also to admit an error as soon as you have proved it to yourself that your idea is wrong. Science is the grave-yard of ideas. . . . But some ideas that seem dead and buried may at one time or another rise up to life again more vital than ever.

Louis Pasteur (1822–1895)

By the year 1800 doctors had many tools that generations earlier had been unknown or little used. They had microscopes to help them study small objects and thermometers to measure temperatures. They had a vaccination technique that just four years earlier had been shown to protect people from smallpox. There were also new medical schools and hospitals populated by a new generation of scientifically minded doctors and students. With all this, medicine was ready to have its greatest century yet.

The Discovery of Anesthetics

One of the century's greatest medical breakthroughs was the discovery of anesthetics—substances that free people from pain during operations. Up until the discovery of anesthetics in the 1840s, surgery was a gruesome experience. Opium, whiskey, and the few other known painkillers were not very good at stopping pain during operations. The following excerpt from a letter written in the 1840s describes the horror of facing an operation in the old days:

> *Before the days of anesthetics a patient preparing for an operation was like a condemned criminal preparing for execution. He counted the days till the appointed day came. He counted the hours of that day till the appointed hour came. He listened for the echo in the street of the surgeon's carriage. He watched for his pull at the door bell, for his foot on the stair, for his step*

in the room, for the production of his dreaded instruments, for his few grave words and his last preparations before beginning; and then he surrendered his liberty and, revolting at the necessity, submitted to be held or bound, and helplessly gave himself up to the cruel knife.

The development of anesthetics—which put an end to such torment — began in 1800. That year the English chemist Sir Humphry Davy (1778–1829) suggested that nitrous oxide (also called *laughing gas*) could be used to help patients avoid pain during operations. Decades passed without much being done about this suggestion, probably because doctors feared harming patients with the gas. Then in the 1840s there was such a burst of interest in anesthetics that historians still disagree on who should be credited with the discovery—Dr. Crawford W. Long, Dr. Horace Wells, Dr. Charles T. Jackson, or Dr. William T. G. Morton.

Crawford Williamson Long (1815–1878) was born in the small town of Danielsville, Georgia, and practiced medicine in the nearby town of Jefferson. Some of the young people in the area liked to attend parties called "happy hours" where they inhaled laughing gas. When Dr. Long was asked to supply laughing gas for a party, he suggested that ether—a sweet-smelling liquid—would be a safe substitute. The young people followed his advice and were soon enjoying what they called "ether frolics." While attending a frolic, Dr. Long observed that those who had sniffed ether could fall or bump into things without seeming to feel pain. He wondered if larger doses of ether could keep patients from feeling pain during operations.

Soon Dr. Long convinced a man with a neck tumor to have it removed while under the influence of ether. On March 30, 1842, Long gave the man ether and then painlessly removed the tumor. Crawford Long was a small-town doctor who preferred hunting and fishing to seeking fame, and he did not realize ether's great potential. Although he performed more operations using ether, Long did not publicize his discovery until 1849, when he published a paper in a medical journal.

Shortly after Dr. Long discovered the benefits of ether, a dentist named Horace Wells (1815–1848) was learning about another possible anesthetic in Hartford, Connecticut. One night in late 1844 Dr. Wells and his wife were attending a stage-show demonstration of laughing gas when the lecturer asked for volunteers. Dr. Wells went up to the stage, inhaled the gas, and began acting silly along with the other volunteers. Fortunately, his mind was clear enough to notice that one volunteer who bumped his legs very hard did not even notice it. Wells wondered if the gas might allow a person to have a tooth painlessly extracted.

It just so happened that Dr. Wells had a tooth that needed to be pulled. On December 11, 1844—the day after the show—Dr. Wells inhaled laughing gas and then had his tooth painlessly removed by another dentist. During the next month Dr. Wells used laughing gas to perform painless dental surgery on at least a dozen other Hartford people.

Unlike Dr. Long, Wells wanted to tell the world about his discovery. In 1845 he went to the Harvard Medical School in Boston, where he gave laughing gas to a patient who then had a tooth pulled. Unfortunately, not enough gas was given to the patient, who yelled out during the operation. Although the patient later said that he had not felt much pain, the procedure was considered a failure. Despite this setback, Wells shared his knowledge with other dentists and doctors in Hartford, and soon laughing gas was being widely used in operations in the Connecticut city.

Meanwhile Charles T. Jackson (1805–1880), a Massachusetts doctor and chemist, was concluding that ether would make a good anesthetic. Dr. Jackson suggested this to William T. G. Morton (1819–1868), a Massachusetts dentist who had studied under Horace Wells and had even been Wells's partner for a while.

Dr. Morton used ether to perform several painless dental operations. Then in the fall of 1846 he successfully administered it to several patients during operations at Massachusetts General Hospital in Boston. One of those patients was a young woman who had a leg

William T. G. Morton demonstrating the use of ether before a group of surgeons at Massachusetts General Hospital in Boston

amputated painlessly. News of Morton's triumphs reached Europe, and soon doctors in many countries were using ether to avoid pain during operations. The American physician and author Dr. Oliver Wendell Holmes (1809–1894) named the process *anesthesia* and the pain-avoiding substances *anesthetics*. He slightly changed the Greek word *anaisthesia*, meaning "insensibility," to coin the two new words.

All four doctors—Crawford W. Long, Horace Wells, Charles T. Jackson, and William T. G. Morton—had contributed to the development of anesthesia. A battle now began over who should receive credit. This battle was probably largely responsible for Dr. Wells's committing suicide three days after his thirty-third birthday, Dr. Morton dying of a seizure at age forty-nine, and Dr. Jackson losing his mind and ending his days in an asylum. Only the quiet Dr. Long lived out a peaceful life. The man who had first used anesthesia without publicizing it died at age sixty-three in Athens, Georgia, while treating a patient.

Despite the disagreements that still persist about who discovered anesthesia, the main fact was that a way had been found to prevent pain during operations. Thanks to ether, laughing gas, and chloroform (first used as an anesthetic by the Scottish doctor Sir James Young Simpson in 1847), many kinds of surgery that had long been impossible could now be attempted. Fortunately, anesthesia came into use in time to help the soldiers of the bloodiest war in United States history—the Civil War, during which half a million men were killed and another half million were wounded.

Germs Cause Disease!

By the early nineteenth century some people realized (as even some ancients had known) that disease strikes more often in dirty places than in clean ones. However, no one knew that this occurs because bacteria, viruses, and other microscopic organisms are more common in filth. Although Leeuwenhoek had first seen bacteria two centuries earlier, no one had yet tied them to disease. And as for viruses, they were much too small to be visible in the microscopes of the time. Edward Jenner had created his smallpox vaccine without knowing that a virus caused the disease.

With so little knowledge about germs, doctors for the most part saw little value in what we consider basic cleanliness. Doctors commonly examined one patient after another without washing their hands or cleaning their instruments. Many even went from examining dead bodies in the morgue to treating patients without washing their hands. As a result, patients often died from infections passed on by the doctors who were supposed to heal them.

The Hungarian physician Ignaz Semmelweis (1818–1865) was one of the first of the nineteenth-century doctors to point out the connection between filth and disease. In 1846 Semmelweis was working at the obstetrics (childbirth) unit of the General Hospital in Vienna, Austria, when he noted a disturbing statistic. Following childbirth, 10 to 30 percent of the new mothers died of *puerperal fever,* an infection of the placental site (tissue connecting the mother to the baby) that often resulted in blood poisoning. Semmelweis was so depressed by the deaths of all those young mothers that he vowed, as he later wrote, "to discover the mysterious agent" that caused puerperal fever.

Semmelweis observed that in the hospital's second ward, where midwives helped the women give birth, the puerperal fever death rate was much lower than in the first ward, where doctors and medical students delivered the babies. What did the doctors and medical students do differently that caused so many of their patients to die?

The midwives usually washed their hands before touching the

women. Not only did many of the doctors and medical students neglect to wash their hands, but they also often examined the women right after dissecting dead bodies. Semmelweis concluded that by not washing their hands the doctors and the medical students were infecting the women with something harmful.

In 1847 Semmelweis ordered those who came into contact with the women to wash their hands thoroughly in disinfectant solution. This reduced the death rate to about 3 percent within a few months. By the next year, 1848, the death rate was cut to about 1 percent.

What a simple solution to a terrible problem! All doctors needed to do to lower the puerperal fever death rate was wash their hands! Semmelweis wrote a book describing his findings. However, instead of adopting his methods, many doctors ridiculed Semmelweis and continued to insist that puerperal fever resulted from poor diet, "bad" air, impure drinking water, or mental depression.

Dismayed at being the butt of jokes, Ignaz Semmelweis called his fellow obstetricians "murderers" of women, left his job in Vienna, and returned to Hungary. Semmelweis's nerves had been wrecked by the battle, though, and he eventually went insane. He was sent

Many doctors opposed Semmelweis's suggestion that they wash their hands with a disinfectant before examining women who had recently given birth.

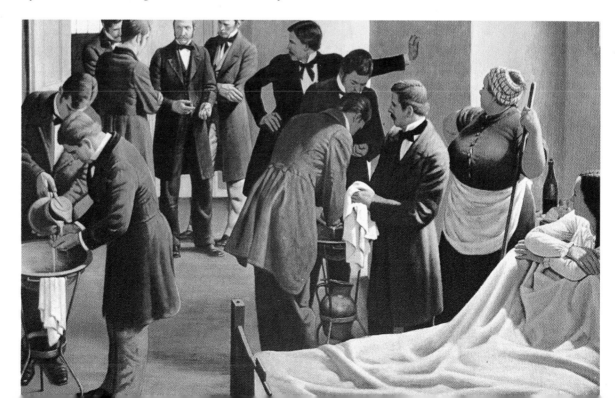

to an asylum, where he died at age forty-seven of blood poisoning—the very disease he had tried to prevent in new mothers.

Several other doctors also made the connection between filth and disease. The Scottish physician Alexander Gordon (1752–1799) understood the link, as did the American doctor and author Oliver Wendell Holmes (1809–1894), who coined the word *anesthesia*. In order to prove that something harmful flourished in filth, however, the nature of germs had to be discovered. Scientists were making steady progress toward this at the very time that Ignaz Semmelweis lay dying in an insane asylum.

During the early 1800s the Italian scientist Agostino Bassi (1773–1856) spent twenty years studying muscardine, a disease affecting silkworms. When Bassi found that a tiny fungus causes muscardine, he became the first person to link a microscopic organism to a disease. After this other scientists, including the great Louis Pasteur (1822–1895), looked for a link between microscopic organisms (also called *microbes* or *germs*) and disease.

Born in Dôle, France, Pasteur first taught school but later became a chemistry professor in Paris. In 1864 he learned that the fermentation that had been ruining large amounts of French wine by making it taste bitter was caused by microbes. He then discovered a way to kill microbes in alcoholic beverages and in milk with heat. Called *pasteurization*, this process is still used to preserve milk, beer, and cheese. Pasteur then turned his attention to the link between microbes and disease in the animal kingdom.

First Pasteur studied anthrax, a disease of people and animals. During the 1840s microscopic, rod-shaped bacteria had been found in the blood of cattle that had died of anthrax. To test his theory that the bacteria caused the disease, in about 1877 Pasteur filtered out the bacteria from anthrax cultures. He took the cultures—which now lacked the bacteria—and injected them into rabbits. When the rabbits did not get anthrax, this implied that the rod-shaped bacteria were responsible for carrying the disease. The German doctor Robert Koch (1843–1910) was also proving that bacteria cause an-

DISCOVERIES OF SOME DISEASE-CAUSING BACTERIA

Disease	Year Germ Discovered
Anthrax	1849
Leprosy	1868
Typhoid fever	1880
Tuberculosis	1882
Cholera	1883
Diphtheria	1883
Tetanus	1884
Pneumonia (most common type)	1886
Salmonella food poisoning	1888
Bubonic plague	1894
Whooping cough	1906

Louis Pasteur (above) working in his lab

thrax at this time. Koch and Pasteur became the first to prove that bacteria can cause a specific disease.

Scientists began studying other kinds of bacteria to see if they caused disease, too. During the late 1800s the microbes that caused numerous diseases including leprosy, typhoid fever, tuberculosis, bacterial pneumonia, and bubonic plague were discovered. Since germs flourished in filth, it became obvious that Ignaz Semmelweis had been right—cleanliness led to better health.

During the late 1800s there was a strong movement throughout the developed countries to promote hygiene (cleanliness) among the public. Washing, bathing, and other germ-killing methods were the main reason that the life expectancy in the United States rose from almost forty to almost fifty years between 1850 and 1900.

More Vaccines

Now that scientists realized that germs cause disease, they began the next logical phase—developing vaccines to prevent disease, as had already been done for smallpox. The problem was that the process by which vaccines work was still a mystery. This mystery was solved by Louis Pasteur, who was observant enough to turn an accident to his advantage.

In 1879, while experimenting with the disease cholera, Pasteur mistakenly injected some old, weakened cholera bacteria into chickens. The bacteria were not strong enough to infect the animals with the disease. However, Pasteur was surprised to find that even when he injected his chickens with fresh, strong cholera bacteria they still remained well. Louis Pasteur realized that the first mild dose had immunized the chickens against cholera, much as cowpox vaccinations immunized people against smallpox. He and Robert Koch, who was doing similar research, became the first to understand that vaccines work by introducing dead or harmless microbes into the body, stimulating the immune system to resist the disease.

Putting this principle into action, in 1881 Pasteur created an anthrax vaccine made of weakened anthrax bacteria. The great French scientist vaccinated a number of animals with it. Protected by their vaccinations, the animals did not get anthrax even when injected with strong doses of the bacteria.

After completing his anthrax vaccine, Pasteur began working on a vaccine against the rare but deadly disease rabies. Carried by a virus that lives in saliva (a secretion in the mouth that begins the digestion of food), rabies is spread by the bite of animals that have the disease. The rabies virus moves along nerves to the spine and the brain. It attacks nerve cells in the brain, killing the victim.

Because the rabies virus was too small to appear in his microscope, Pasteur could not track down the cause of the disease. However, he reasoned that whatever caused rabies had to settle in the central nervous system (the brain and spinal cord). A proof of this was that if brain pieces from rabies victims were injected into healthy animals, the animals developed rabies. Pasteur then thought of an ingenious way of creating a rabies vaccine using central nervous system material from rabies victims.

Pasteur removed the spinal cords of rabbits that had died of rabies. He learned that the longer the cords were left to dry, the weaker the rabies virus inside them became. Pasteur decided to experiment on dogs. He vaccinated dogs with cord that was fourteen days old, then with thirteen-day-old cord, and so on until he had injected them with material from a fresh cord. Hoping that he had stimulated the dogs' immune systems to gradually build resistance to rabies, Pasteur then injected a deadly rabies dose into the animals. When the dogs weren't harmed, Pasteur knew that his method worked.

The rabies vaccine could not be put into general use among human beings for several reasons. First, there is some danger in vaccination. Should too strong a dose be given, instead of building resistance to the disease. If rabies were common, the few people who might get the disease from the vaccine would be more than offset by the thousands whose lives would be saved by it. Rabies is so rare, however, that it wasn't worth the risk. Unlike the smallpox vaccine

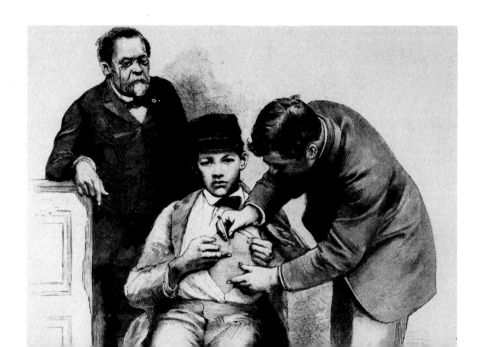

Pasteur's successful discovery of a vaccine against rabies inspired other scientists to develop vaccines for diphtheria and typhoid fever.

risk. Unlike the smallpox vaccine that was used to prevent the disease among the general public, the rabies vaccine was only for those who had already been bitten by a rabid animal.

Pasteur's first chance to use his vaccine came in July of 1885, when Joseph Meister, a boy who had been bitten by a rabid dog, was brought to the scientist by his frantic parents. Pasteur gave Joseph a series of thirteen increasingly stronger doses of rabies vaccine. The boy built up immunity to rabies before the disease could infect him, and he fought it off. Soon after this, Pasteur successfully vaccinated a man who had been bitten by a rabid dog while keeping it away from a group of children. Within a few years nearly twenty-five hundred people had been saved from rabies by the Pasteur vaccine. The same basic method is used to ward off the disease today.

Louis Pasteur had shown that an intelligent scientist needed little more than a few experimental animals, a supply of germs, and some inexpensive lab equipment to create a disease-preventing vaccine. Inspired by his work, scientists attempted to develop vaccines for other diseases. Among other vaccines developed in the nineteenth century were ones for diphtheria and typhoid fever.

Saving Lives in the Operating Room

The knowledge that germs cause disease saved lives in several ways. It enabled people to avoid disease simply by keeping themselves and their dwellings cleaner. It allowed doctors to develop vaccines and drugs against specific germs. Knowledge about germs also saved countless lives in the operating room.

The discovery of anesthesia allowed surgeons of the 1850s and 1860s to do many more operations than they could do in the past. Even when the surgery was successful, however, many patients died of infections following the operations. The problem was that most operating rooms were filthy by today's standards. While the patients' bodies were open, the germs in the operating room had access to their internal organs. Largely because of unsanitary conditions, until the late 1800s, half of all operations resulted in death.

Joseph Lister

Joseph Lister (1827–1912), an English surgeon working in Glasgow, Scotland, was among those appalled by all the surgical deaths. Even before it was proved, Lister believed that infections were caused by germs. He experimented with various substances that might kill germs in the operating room. After his tests showed that carbolic acid would work, Lister decided to try it on a patient.

On August 12, 1865, Lister prepared to treat a patient with a compound fracture—one in which bone fragments protrude through the skin. In the past, such fractures had often ended with the limb having to be amputated because of infection. Lister sprayed the patient and the operating room with carbolic acid and then successfully repaired the fracture—a success that was soon repeated in other operations. To describe germ-killing with chemicals, scientists combined the Greek words *anti* (against) and *sepsis* (decay) to make the word *antiseptic*. Lister soon improved antiseptic surgery by killing germs on the surgeon's hands and on the instruments and surgical dressings. He also discovered better germ-killing agents than carbolic acid.

Like Ignaz Semmelweis, Lister at first met with opposition, especially in London where he took a post as professor of surgery. But as Lister's method continued to save lives and as more was learned about germs, the medical world was won over. Sir Joseph Lister's creation of antiseptic surgery has saved untold millions of lives the world over.

During the 1880s and 1890s some surgeons realized that, in addition to killing germs in the operating room, it would be very beneficial to try to keep germs out in the first place. Instruments were sterilized before they reached the operating room. The clothing of surgeons and nurses and operating room materials were also kept as free of germs as possible. This method of keeping germs out of the operating room is called *aseptic* (meaning "not decayed") *surgery.* Today aseptic methods are used to keep germs out of operating rooms, and antiseptics are used to kill any germs that might get in anyway.

New Instruments Lead to Specialization

The nineteenth century was the golden age of inventing. Among the century's creations were the steam locomotive (1804), photography (1826), matches (about 1827), the telegraph (1836), the sewing machine (1846), the internal-combustion engine (1860), the telephone (1876), the phonograph (1877), the electric light (1879), the gasoline automobile (1885), the diesel engine (1892), and the radio (1895). Quite a few medical tools were also created during the nineteenth century.

Up until the early 1800s, doctors listened to their patients' hearts

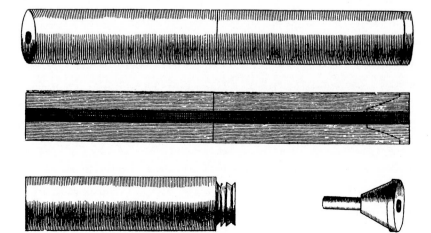

Laënnec's stethoscope

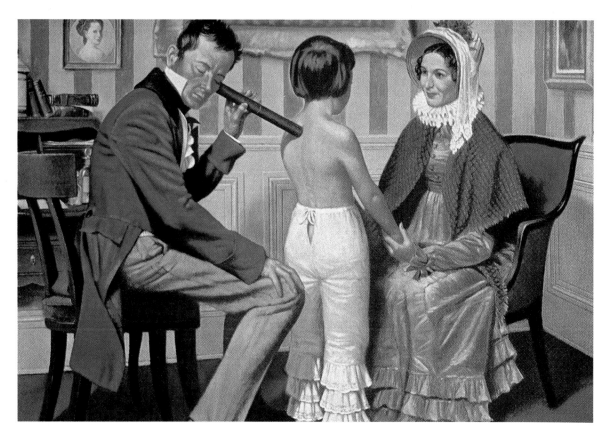

and other organs by placing their ears against the people's bodies. In 1816 the French physician René Laënnec (1781–1826) invented the stethoscope so that doctors could listen to patients' inside organs more effectively. The stethoscope consists of earpieces, hollow tubing, and a contact piece that picks up sounds from the patient.

Many more of today's instruments also originated during the 1800s. In 1851 the German scientist Hermann von Helmholtz (1821–1894) invented the ophthalmoscope, an instrument for studying the inside of the eye. In 1853 a device for giving "shots," the hypodermic syringe, was invented by the French doctor Charles Pravaz and the Scottish doctor Alexander Wood. In 1876 an instrument for studying the bladder, the cystoscope, was invented; and in 1898 came the bronchoscope, an instrument for examining the insides of the bronchial tubes (breathing passages).

Laënnec's stethoscope and his published reports on its use helped physicians to better understand pulmonary diseases—especially tuberculosis, the condition which eventually led to the death of Laënnec himself.

Wilhelm Roentgen demonstrated his X-ray machine on January 23, 1896.

One of the most amazing breakthroughs in the history of medicine occurred near the end of the century in 1895. That year the German physicist Wilhelm Konrad Roentgen (1845–1923) discovered a form of energy that could penetrate solid substances and reveal what was inside them. Because Roentgen did not know much about these rays at first, he named them *X rays.* Soon doctors were building X-ray machines and using them to look for signs of disease inside patients' bodies.

Before the 1800s, a doctor had typically practiced many kinds of medicine. He delivered babies; performed simple surgery; cared for eye, bladder, and digestive problems; treated the diseases of the very young and the very old; and tried to help people with mental illnesses. By the end of the nineteenth century it had become difficult for one person to master all the complex devices that had recently been invented. It was also impossible for one person to keep track of all the new discoveries that were being made in the various medical fields. For these reasons, nineteenth century doctors began

specializing in a single branch of medicine. Among the specialties were ophthalmology (the eyes), radiology (the use of X rays), and public health (sanitation and other basic medical problems of a community).

In the one glorious century between 1800 and 1900 more major medical advances had been made than had occurred in the entire previous history of mankind. Thanks to all these advances, between 1800 and 1900 the average life span in developed countries increased more than ten years to nearly fifty years. Not only that, but in 1800 one-half of the children had died from disease before age five; by 1900, the figure had gone down to about one-fourth of the children dying before their fifth birthdays.

To us, an average life span of only fifty years sounds too short, and one-fourth of the children dying before age five seems outrageous. Doctors had much to learn about disease and how to prevent and cure it before people could live the long and generally healthy lives enjoyed by most of us today.

Chapter 6
From 1900 to the Present

Never neglect any appearance or any happening which seems to be out of the ordinary: more often than not it is a false alarm, but it may be an important truth.

Alexander Fleming (1881–1955),
discoverer of penicillin

Vitamins

In 1906 the English scientist Sir Frederick Gowland Hopkins (1861–1947) performed a diet experiment on rats. He refined the proteins, fats, and carbohydrates out of the rats' usual food. Then he fed the animals only the proteins, fats, and carbohydrates. It was thought that these substances had enough nutrients to keep the rats healthy. However, when the animals became ill, Hopkins knew that some vital nutrients had been lost when he'd filtered everything out of their food except the proteins, fats, and carbohydrates.

Hopkins called these unknown nutrients "accessory food factors." A few years later, in 1912, the Polish American biochemist Casimir Funk (1884–1967) referred to them as "vitamines." When the final *e* was dropped from *vitamines* in 1920, these substances became known as *vitamins*.

Thirteen vitamins, each with a key role in health maintenance, have been discovered in this century. Too little of any vitamin—and in many cases too much—can result in illness. For example, not enough vitamin C can bring on scurvy, a disease involving gum bleeding, loss of teeth, sore joints, and skin rashes. It has long been known that sailors away at sea and others who went long periods without certain fruits and vegetables were prone to scurvy. However, only in this century have scientists learned that these fruits and vegetables contain a substance needed by the body: vitamin C.

Eight separate vitamins make up the vitamin B complex, and too

little of any of them can cause problems. Lack of vitamin B$_1$ can bring on beriberi, a disease that causes heart failure, mental changes, anemia, and even numbness and paralysis. Lack of vitamin B$_2$ leads to eye and skin problems and mouth soreness. Not enough niacin causes pellagra, a disease in which the victims suffer from a dark scaly rash, diarrhea, and mental changes. Not enough vitamin B$_6$ can lead to nervous system problems, and lack of vitamin B$_{12}$ can cause anemia.

Once doctors realized that vitamin deficiencies caused these and other diseases, medicine had a powerful new weapon. All that was needed to cure people of certain health problems was to provide doses of the missing vitamins. Today, all of the thirteen vitamins are available in pill form. In some poor countries where people lack vitamins, the governments supply vitamin tablets to the public.

Dr. James Lind's experiments on British sailors in the 1700s proved that eating citrus fruits would cure scurvy.

Viruses Revealed!

During the 1890s doctors had been unable to find the causes of several diseases. Thinking that unknown bacteria were to blame, they built filters with openings small enough to trap bacteria. When fluids infected by these diseases were poured through these filters, however, bacteria were not trapped. The agents causing the diseases had passed right through the filters, meaning that they were much smaller than bacteria! Although the microscopes of the time could not reveal these unknown organisms, they were given the Latin name *viruses*, meaning "poisons."

The improved microscopes of the twentieth century enabled scientists to see viruses for the first time in 1925. Shortly after that, in the early 1930s, an extremely powerful instrument, the electron microscope, was developed. Able to magnify objects more than a hundred thousand times, electron microscopes revealed that viruses typically have a diameter less than a tenth of that of bacteria. Diseases found to be caused by viruses include yellow fever, chicken pox, mumps, influenza, rabies, polio, and the common cold.

Just as identifying bacteria enabled nineteenth-century scientists to create vaccines against bacterial diseases, twentieth-century scientists have been able to develop vaccines against several virus diseases. Among the vaccines developed in this century were ones for yellow fever in 1937, influenza in 1943, polio in 1955, measles in 1963, and mumps in 1969.

The Wonder Drugs

It has long been known that certain chemicals are useful in treating certain diseases. Quinine, an anti-malaria drug (still in use) made from cinchona tree bark, was discovered by South American Indians hundreds of years ago. Mercury, an element used in thermometers, was first directed against the sexually transmitted disease syphilis in the 1400s or earlier. In the centuries following the discovery of quinine and mercury, not much progress in the development of drugs occurred. By the year 1900 only the painkiller morphine, the mild pain reliever aspirin, the antiseptic iodine, and a few other substances had been added to the arsenal of useful drugs. In fact, nearly all of the drugs prescribed today were developed in this very century.

The use of drugs to combat disease is called *chemotherapy.* The German scientist Paul Ehrlich (1854–1915) is called the "founder of chemotherapy," because he was the first to search for disease-fighting chemicals in the systematic way used today. In 1910 Ehrlich was testing his 606th chemical combination against the disease syphilis when he finally met with success. This drug, called Salvarsan, or "606," was the biggest advance in the fight against syphilis since mercury had been found to help relieve the disease's symptoms near the end of the Middle Ages. Soon Ehrlich discovered a related compound, Neosalvarsan or "914," that was better than Salvarsan because it was less harmful to healthy tissue. This is still the goal of drug researchers—to find medicines that attack disease and its causes while leaving healthy tissue unharmed.

In 1908 Ehrlich and Metchnikoff shared a Nobel Prize for their outstanding work in immunology.

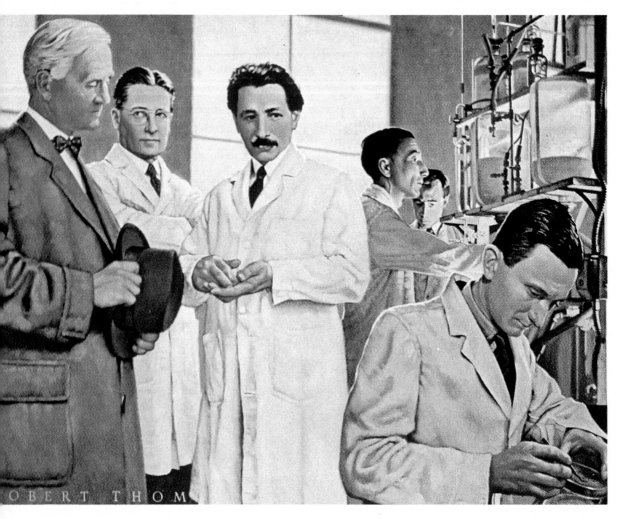

OBERT THOM

By the 1940s Dr. Alexander Fleming (center) and U.S. scientists were able to produce penicillin on a massive scale. It completely revolutionized the practice of medicine.

One of the most important of today's drugs was discovered by a scientist who, like Pasteur with his cholera experiment, took advantage of an accident. In 1928 the Scottish-born bacteriologist Alexander Fleming (1881–1955) was growing a staphylococci bacteria culture in his London laboratory when a mold blew in through the window and landed on his culture plate. Examining the plate, Fleming was amazed to find that the bacteria—which caused such serious diseases as pneumonia and blood poisoning—were being killed by the mold! Further experiments revealed that the mold, *Penicillium notatum*, produced a substance that destroyed certain disease-causing bacteria. He named the mold's bacteria-killing substance *penicillin* and predicted that one day it would "come into its own as a therapeutic agent."

Penicillin was the first of the antibiotics—drugs that use one organism to fight another. The problem was that for years scientists couldn't concentrate enough penicillin from the crude mold to make the drug useful. When scientists finally learned to produce large amounts of penicillin in the 1940s, the drug was unleashed against a long list of bacterial diseases including pneumonia, strep throat, scarlet fever, blood poisoning, and syphilis.

In 1943 the Russian-American scientist Selman Waksman (1888–1973) discovered streptomycin, a powerful antibiotic made from a microbe that grows in soil. In the years since the discovery of penicillin and streptomycin, more than sixty other antibiotics have been found to help cure numerous bacterial diseases. Because they save thousands of lives daily in all corners of our world, antibiotics are often called "wonder drugs," "miracle drugs," and "the medical breakthrough of the twentieth century." Antibiotics are a main reason why people in developed countries now live an average of more than twenty-five years longer than people did a century ago.

Following Dr. Selman Waksman's discovery of streptomycin, more than sixty other drugs were discovered to treat bacterial diseases.

Advances in the Treatment of Mental Illness

There have always been people who cannot cope with daily life. For most of our history, treatment of the mentally ill has been terrible. As recently as four hundred years ago many mentally ill people spent their lives in prisons or in dungeon-like asylums where they were chained up like animals. London had a famous asylum known as *Bedlam* (officially Saint Mary of Bethlehem) where patients were displayed like sideshow freaks. Just as we go to the zoo for entertainment, Londoners visited Bedlam to watch the patients' antics.

One reason for this cruelty was the belief that mentally ill people were possessed by the devil. The French prison doctor Philippe Pinel (1745–1826) was one of the first to insist that mental patients were sick and needed treatment. Pinel convinced authorities that mental patients need not be chained up unless they were violent. The American reformer Dorothea Dix (1802–1887) was one of the

The painting shows Philippe Pinel releasing mental patients from their chains.

first to champion the rights of mental patients in the United States. Upset that the mentally ill were often imprisoned alongside criminals, Dix helped establish mental hospitals in fifteen states of the United States and also in Canada, Europe, and Japan.

More humane treatment of mental patients was vital, but progress in preventing and curing mental illnesses could not be made until their causes were understood. Fortunately, during the late 1800s Sigmund Freud (1856–1939) appeared on the scene. Between about 1890 and his death half a century later this Austrian doctor probably revealed more about the human mind than had been learned in all previous centuries.

Freud helped found psychiatry, the branch of medicine dealing with mental disorders. He showed that mental problems are triggered by certain events, often dating from childhood. Freud also proved that various treatments can relieve mental problems and demonstrated that psychoanalysis (a treatment method in which patients talk about their mental problems to understand them better) helps many patients. During the years since Freud's death, psychiatry has been revolutionized by new drugs and therapies. All this progress was made possible by Sigmund Freud and several other psychiatric pioneers who brought mental illness out into the open and began studying it scientifically.

The Conquest of Polio

Communicable diseases are ones that can be passed from person to person. By the early 1950s, medicine had made great progress in preventing and/or curing smallpox, pneumonia, diphtheria, strep throat, syphilis, whooping cough, scarlet fever, tuberculosis, and many other communicable diseases. Polio, an inflammation of the brain and spinal cord that can result in paralysis and even death, was a major exception. As recently as 1952 a polio epidemic struck fifty thousand Americans, killing thirty-three hundred of them. Millions of people now living—perhaps your own parents— remember the terror that polio once inspired.

Polio was so difficult to conquer because it is caused by a virus. The antibiotics and other major drugs that are effective against bacteria are helpless against most viruses. Polio researchers reasoned that they had little hope of soon finding a drug that would kill the polio virus, and even today no drug can cure polio once a person is sick with it. Instead, researchers knew that their best hope was to develop a vaccine to prevent polio.

The polio virus had been known since the early 1900s. However, for many years doctors could not weaken the virus to the point where it could provoke an immune response without causing polio. In 1953 the American scientist Jonas Salk (born in 1914) finally found a way to kill the polio virus without destroying its ability to stimulate an immune response. Dr. Salk made a vaccine out of the dead polio viruses and tried it on his own family and a few others. The vaccine passed all tests, including a massive one done in 1954 on nearly two million schoolchildren. In 1955 the Salk vaccine was pronounced a success, and Jonas Salk was hailed as one of the world's great medical heroes.

As far as the world's children were concerned, the only bad part of the Salk vaccine was that it was given as a "shot." When the American medical researcher Dr. Albert Sabin (born in 1906) developed an oral liquid polio vaccine in 1960, children were much happier. Not only was the Sabin vaccine drunk instead of given as a

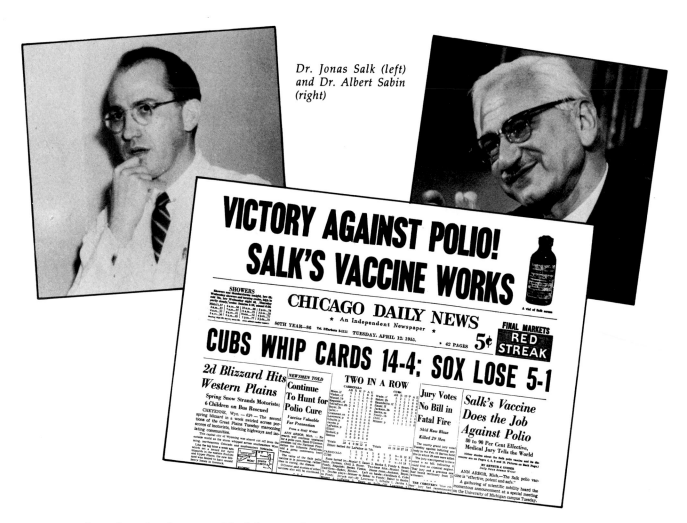

Dr. Jonas Salk (left) and Dr. Albert Sabin (right)

shot, but it also provided longer-lasting protection. Together, the Salk and Sabin vaccines have prevented hundreds of thousands of people in all corners of the world from getting polio.

Surgical Breakthroughs

In the middle of the twentieth century surgeons learned to operate on organs that had been off-limits a few years earlier. One of the main such advances was open-heart surgery, which was begun in the 1940s. During an open-heart operation, the surgeon can open the chest and then repair the heart. Open-heart surgery was made possible by the development of the heart-lung machine that takes over the job of the heart and lungs during such operations.

One heart operation that has become routine in recent years is called the coronary artery bypass. The bypass is done when fatty deposits form in the arteries, causing them to narrow. The narrow arteries do not allow enough blood to reach the heart, and this lack of blood prevents the heart from pumping properly. During a bypass, the surgeon takes either a piece of vein from the patient's leg or the internal mammary artery from inside the chest and uses it to create a new route for the blood on its way to the heart.

Until recently, people whose hearts or other vital organs were too damaged to be repaired simply died. Today many people with faulty organs can have them replaced with organs taken from either living or dead people. The first successful major organ transplant was performed in 1954, when a man with a fatal kidney disease was given a kidney from his twin brother. The patient lived for eight years. Since then, surgeons have learned to transplant the heart, pancreas, liver, bone marrow, and heart-and-lungs combination.

The first heart transplant was performed on December 3, 1967, by Dr. Christiaan N. Barnard (born in 1922 in South Africa). Dr. Barnard took the heart of a twenty-five-year-old woman who had died in a car crash and placed it in the chest of Louis Washkansky, a fifty-five-year-old grocer whose own heart was malfunctioning. Although his new heart was still working, Washkansky died of other problems eighteen days later. Since then, hundreds of people have had heart transplants. Nearly half of them have lived for at least five years following their operations.

Dr. Christiaan Barnard

In the early years of organ transplantation, there was one major problem. The body's immune system, which has the job of resisting invasions by foreign substances, often treated the new organs as foreign objects and rejected them. As a result, patients with perfectly good new organs died. A major breakthrough with the rejection problem occurred in the early 1980s, when the drug cyclosporine was introduced. Obtained from fungi, cyclosporine stops the immune system from rejecting newly implanted organs but does not stop the system from rejecting truly harmful substances such as bacteria. Since the discovery of this drug, the success rate for organ transplantation has greatly improved.

Better Health Care for the Poor

Many major medical improvements have been made during the twentieth century. Great progress has been made in cancer detection and treatment. Machines have been devised that can reveal the brain's inner workings or the sex of an unborn child. As a result of all the new medical technologies, people in the developed nations now live to an average age of about seventy-five.

The story is much different in the world's poor, undeveloped nations. The poor countries have a shortage of doctors, nurses, and hospitals. They lack vaccines to prevent diseases and drugs to treat the sick. Millions of human beings in the poor nations (perhaps 30 percent of all the people in the world) do not even have enough food to maintain decent health. As a result, the people in many poor countries live to an average age of only about forty.

Decent medical care is gradually being introduced in the poor nations. Millions of people in those countries are now receiving vaccinations and basic health care for the first time. Several United Nations agencies and other health organizations are working to do this, and the governments of some wealthy countries are also helping. Although the death toll from disease is still shockingly high in the undeveloped nations, progress is being made in bringing twentieth-century medicine to the poor people of the world.

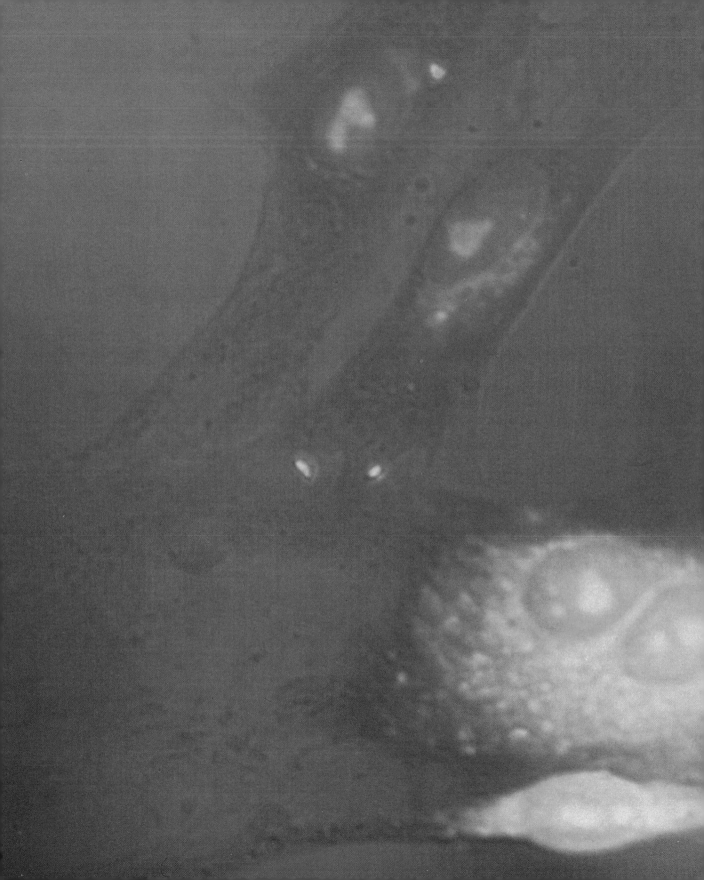

PART II: TODAY

Light micrograph of human nerve cells

Chapter 7
The Human Body

What a piece of work is a man! [*Author's note:* or a woman!]

William Shakespeare

To do their jobs, mathematicians must know about numbers, geologists must know the Earth's history, and chemists must understand how substances interact. In the same way, medical people must be familiar with the human body. Before looking at present-day medicine it will help if you know about the body, too.

Because nearly every part has a vital job, the body is often compared to a complex machine. Actually, it is more accurate to say that a machine is like the body. After all, human bodies were working quite well a million years before the first machine was invented!

The Brain

The thinking organ, called the brain, is the body's irreplaceable part. If you had a heart transplant, you would still be you. In fact, if every other organ except your brain were replaced, you would still have your identity. But without your brain you wouldn't exist, because your brain *is* you.

The brain is not impressive in size or appearance. At six years of age, when it stops growing in size, the human brain weighs about three pounds and looks like a large cauliflower. Yet the brain is the most amazing and complex object known in the universe.

The brain gathers information from the outside world, interprets it, and then decides how to respond. The brain also tells the mouth what to say (or not say), controls all the workings of the body, stores memories, and is responsible for our creative abilities. The expression "have a heart" should really be "have a brain," because the brain and not the heart is the seat of love and all our other emotions. These separate functions are controlled by parts of the brain.

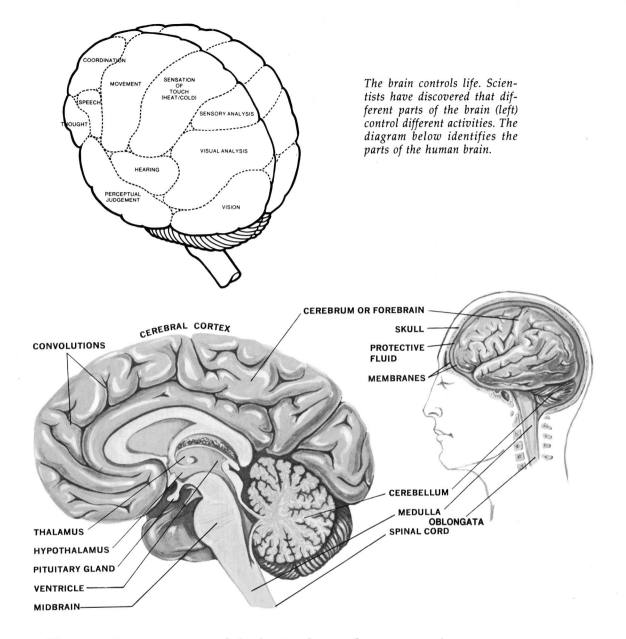

The brain controls life. Scientists have discovered that different parts of the brain (left) control different activities. The diagram below identifies the parts of the human brain.

COORDINATION
MOVEMENT
SENSATION OF TOUCH (HEAT/COLD)
SPEECH
SENSORY ANALYSIS
THOUGHT
VISUAL ANALYSIS
HEARING
PERCEPTUAL JUDGEMENT
VISION

CONVOLUTIONS
CEREBRAL CORTEX
CEREBRUM OR FOREBRAIN
SKULL
PROTECTIVE FLUID
MEMBRANES
THALAMUS
HYPOTHALAMUS
PITUITARY GLAND
VENTRICLE
MIDBRAIN
CEREBELLUM
MEDULLA OBLONGATA
SPINAL CORD

The most important part of the brain, the cerebrum, comprises about 85 percent of total brain weight. The cerebrum is the center of consciousness and memory. It also controls the skeletal muscles and receives messages relating to sight, taste, smell, hearing, and touch. The cerebrum is divided into two parts, or cerebral hemispheres. The left hemisphere controls the right side of the body, while the right hemisphere controls the left side. The left hemisphere is usually dominant, which is why most of us are right-handed.

Beneath the two cerebral hemispheres is the mushroom-shaped brain area called the cerebellum, which controls balance and coordinates the movement of various body parts. Near the cerebellum is the pyramid-shaped medulla oblongata, the control center for heartbeat, breathing, swallowing, and vomiting. Deep within the brain is the hypothalamus, the controller of several emotions, especially anger and fear, and of body temperature, hunger, and thirst. Not involved in any thought processes are three protective membranes, or meninges, that surround the brain.

Although scientists know much about the jobs of the various brain parts, they know little about how the brain works, why brains vary in abilities, and how they give us our consciousness and individuality. In fact, the more that is learned about the brain the more questions arise about it, so that in some ways the brain is as mysterious today as it was to ancient people.

The Rest of the Nervous System

The brain is the main part of the nervous system—the complex network that keeps us in contact with the outside world and also keeps our organs working properly. The nervous system has three major aspects: (1) the central nervous system, (2) the peripheral nervous system, and (3) the autonomic nervous system.

The central nervous system consists of the brain and the spinal cord—a long, thick bundle of nerves extending from the base of the brain down through the backbone. The central nervous system does the thinking and is in overall charge of the body's activities.

The peripheral nervous system carries messages from the body to the spinal cord and then to the brain and from the brain and spinal cord back to the body. It does this along forty-three pairs of nerves connecting various body parts to the brain and the spinal cord.

The autonomic nervous system directs breathing and other automatic bodily processes. It consists of numerous nerves connecting the central nervous system to the organs. You need not think about breathing or digesting your food because the autonomic nervous

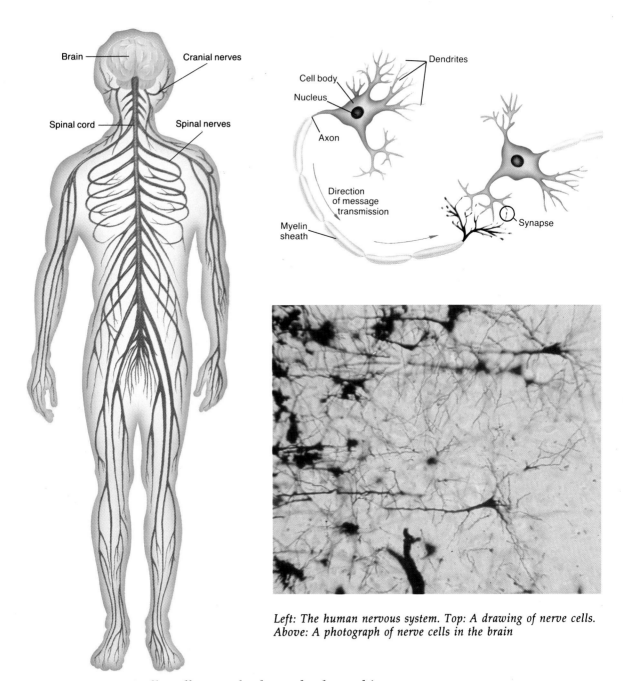

Left: *The human nervous system. Top: A drawing of nerve cells.*
Above: A photograph of nerve cells in the brain

system automatically tells your body to do these things.

The building blocks of the nervous system are billions of nerve cells called neurons (bundles of which are called nerves). Neurons carry information from the sensory organs to the brain, from the brain to the muscles, and also within the brain and spinal cord.

73

Sense Organs

Without eyes you could not enjoy the blue of the sky. Without taste buds and a nose you wouldn't notice much difference between a roast beef sandwich and one made of cardboard. Without ears you couldn't hear music, and with no sense of touch, how would you paint a picture or enjoy a hug?

Our sense organs keep us in contact with the outside world. The five senses are seeing, hearing, touching, tasting, and smelling. The organs that gather sensory information are the eyes, ears, skin, taste buds, and nose. Information gathered by these sense organs travels along nerves to the brain, where it is interpreted.

Eyes are the organs for seeing. The eye parts include the cornea and the lens, which help the eye focus; the iris, which regulates the amount of light entering the eye; the pupil, the opening in the iris that changes size depending on how much light the iris is letting in;

THE EYE

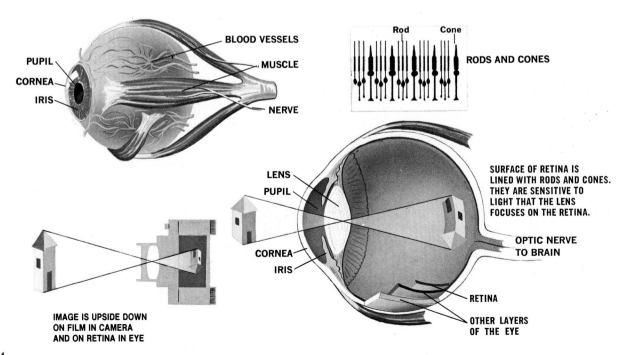

BLOOD VESSELS
MUSCLE
NERVE
PUPIL
CORNEA
IRIS

Rod   Cone
RODS AND CONES

LENS
PUPIL
CORNEA
IRIS

SURFACE OF RETINA IS LINED WITH RODS AND CONES. THEY ARE SENSITIVE TO LIGHT THAT THE LENS FOCUSES ON THE RETINA.

OPTIC NERVE TO BRAIN

RETINA

OTHER LAYERS OF THE EYE

IMAGE IS UPSIDE DOWN ON FILM IN CAMERA AND ON RETINA IN EYE

and the retina, which forms the image of what the eye is looking at. The two retinas create upside-down images. Information regarding these images is sent through the optic nerves to the brain, which produces the right-side-up picture that you see.

Ears are the organs for sensing sound waves. The ear parts include the external auditory canal, the opening leading into the ear portions within the head; the eardrum, a tissue that vibrates when struck by sound waves and which then sets three bones called auditory ossicles to vibrating; and the organ of Corti, the part that does the actual hearing. Information on the vibrations sensed by the organ of Corti is sent by the auditory nerves to the brain. The brain then converts the message into the sounds you hear. Within each ear are also three semicircular canals that help us keep our balance.

The largest organ of your body, the skin, is actually on the outside. Skin contains nerve endings that are sensitive to pressure. Impulses from the nerve endings travel to your brain where they are interpreted as the sense of touch. Your skin also helps protect your internal organs.

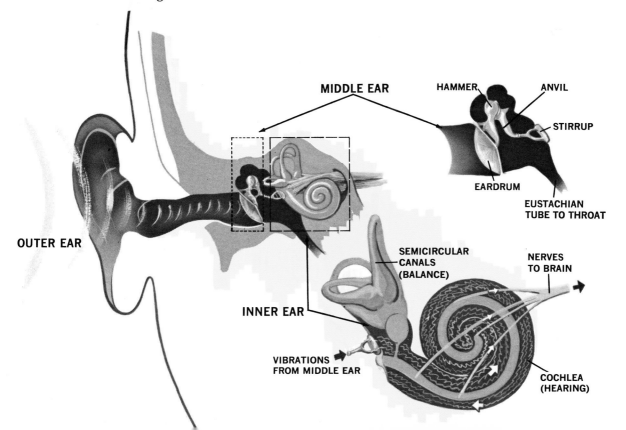

MIDDLE EAR

HAMMER

ANVIL

STIRRUP

EARDRUM

EUSTACHIAN TUBE TO THROAT

OUTER EAR

SEMICIRCULAR CANALS (BALANCE)

NERVES TO BRAIN

INNER EAR

VIBRATIONS FROM MIDDLE EAR

COCHLEA (HEARING)

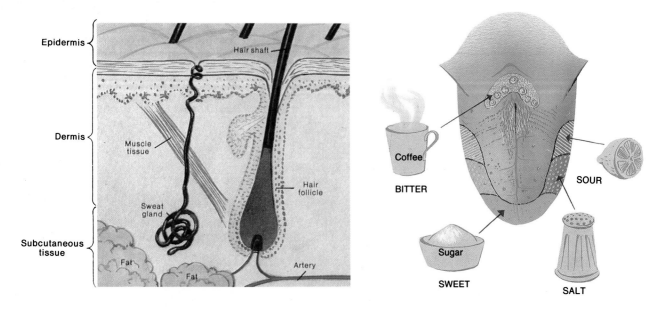

Epidermis

Hair shaft

Dermis

Muscle tissue

Sweat gland

Hair follicle

Subcutaneous tissue

Fat

Fat

Artery

Coffee

BITTER

Sugar

SWEET

SOUR

SALT

Above: Drawing of skin. Right: Four kinds of taste buds are located on different areas of the tongue.

The sense of taste is provided by thousands of taste buds on the tongue. Clusters of taste buds on various parts of the tongue are sensitive to different tastes, such as salty, sour, bitter, and sweet. As you eat, the taste buds send information by way of special nerves to your brain. The brain sorts the information out into various tastes.

Many organs have more than one purpose. Such is the case with the nose, the organ for both breathing and smelling. Smells are created by chemical gases given off by substances. These gases make their way high up into your nose where they stimulate special odor-detecting cells. These cells send their messages along the two olfactory nerves to your brain, which then makes you aware of the various odors.

The Skeleton

A house or apartment has a framework that supports the entire structure. The body has a similar framework, called the skeleton, that protects the internal organs and helps hold the body together.

The human skeleton is composed of about two hundred and six bones. The word *about* is used, because the number varies. A child's spinal column has bones that join together in adulthood, resulting

HUMAN SKELETON

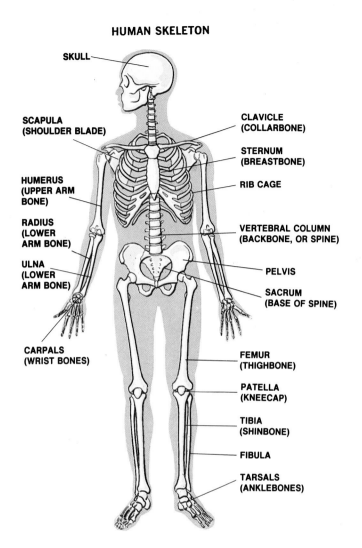

SKULL

SCAPULA
(SHOULDER BLADE)

CLAVICLE
(COLLARBONE)

STERNUM
(BREASTBONE)

HUMERUS
(UPPER ARM
BONE)

RIB CAGE

RADIUS
(LOWER
ARM BONE)

VERTEBRAL COLUMN
(BACKBONE, OR SPINE)

ULNA
(LOWER
ARM BONE)

PELVIS

SACRUM
(BASE OF SPINE)

CARPALS
(WRIST BONES)

FEMUR
(THIGHBONE)

PATELLA
(KNEECAP)

TIBIA
(SHINBONE)

FIBULA

TARSALS
(ANKLEBONES)

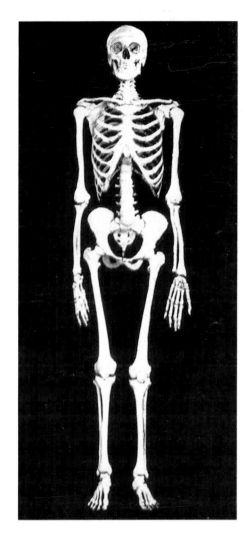

in a numerical change within a person's lifetime. In addition, some
people have extra fingers and toes. However, most adults have
twenty-nine bones in the skull (head), twenty-four ribs, twenty-six
vertebrae (bones in the back), twenty-seven bones in each hand,
twenty-six per foot, three in each leg, three per arm, two collar-
bones, two shoulder blades, two kneecaps, a breastbone, and two
hipbones—making a total of two hundred and six.

Made largely of the minerals calcium and phosphorus and the
protein collagen, bones are among the body's hardest parts. Bones
are hollow in the middle, though. Inside bone cavities is a tissue
called marrow, where blood cells are made.

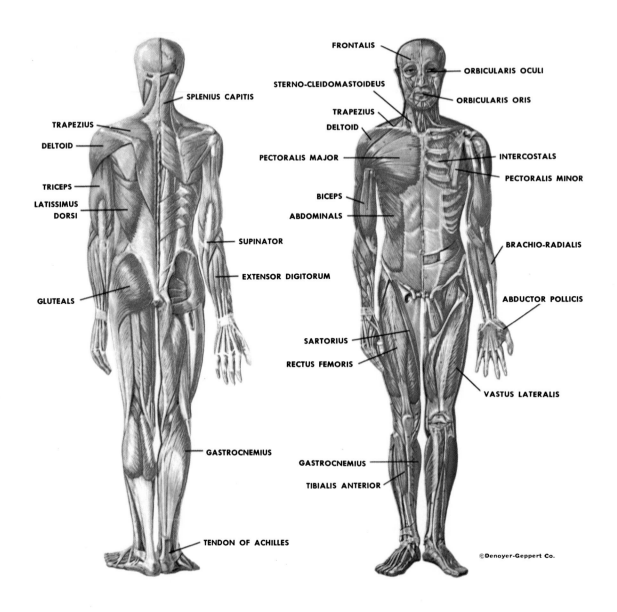

FRONTALIS
ORBICULARIS OCULI
STERNO-CLEIDOMASTOIDEUS
ORBICULARIS ORIS
TRAPEZIUS
DELTOID
PECTORALIS MAJOR
INTERCOSTALS
PECTORALIS MINOR
BICEPS
ABDOMINALS
BRACHIO-RADIALIS
ABDUCTOR POLLICIS
SARTORIUS
RECTUS FEMORIS
VASTUS LATERALIS
GASTROCNEMIUS
TIBIALIS ANTERIOR

SPLENIUS CAPITIS
TRAPEZIUS
DELTOID
TRICEPS
LATISSIMUS DORSI
SUPINATOR
EXTENSOR DIGITORUM
GLUTEALS
GASTROCNEMIUS
TENDON OF ACHILLES

©Denoyer-Geppert Co.

The Muscles

Attached to the bones and organs are more than six hundred and fifty muscles—tissues that make the body move. There are two main kinds of muscles—skeletal and smooth.

Skeletal muscles are attached to the bones and enable the bones to move. For example, the twenty-seven bones in each of your hands are moved by thirty-five muscles, and your facial expression is controlled by dozens of muscles. The skeletal muscles are voluntary, meaning that a person decides when to use them. Smooth muscles, on the other hand, are involuntary, meaning that they work automatically. The smooth muscles help propel substances through various organs, such as blood through the veins and food through the stomach and intestines.

One special muscle looks like a skeletal muscle but works automatically like a smooth one. This unique muscle is the heart—the center of the circulatory system.

The Circulatory System

The body is made of more than 10 trillion (10,000,000,000,000) cells. All of these microscopic units need oxygen and food. They also must rid themselves of waste products. A special fluid called blood does these jobs for the cells, and also fights germs that attack the body.

Blood has four main components: red blood cells (erythrocytes), white blood cells (leukocytes), platelets, and plasma. Red blood cells carry oxygen from the lungs to various parts of the body and

The drawing (bottom left) and photograph (bottom right) show the three types of cells present in all human blood.

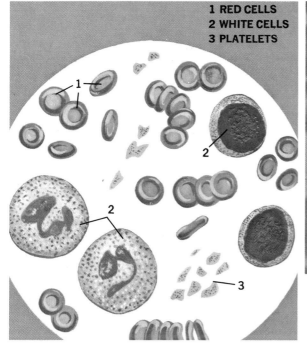

1 RED CELLS
2 WHITE CELLS
3 PLATELETS

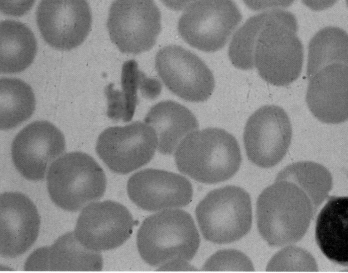

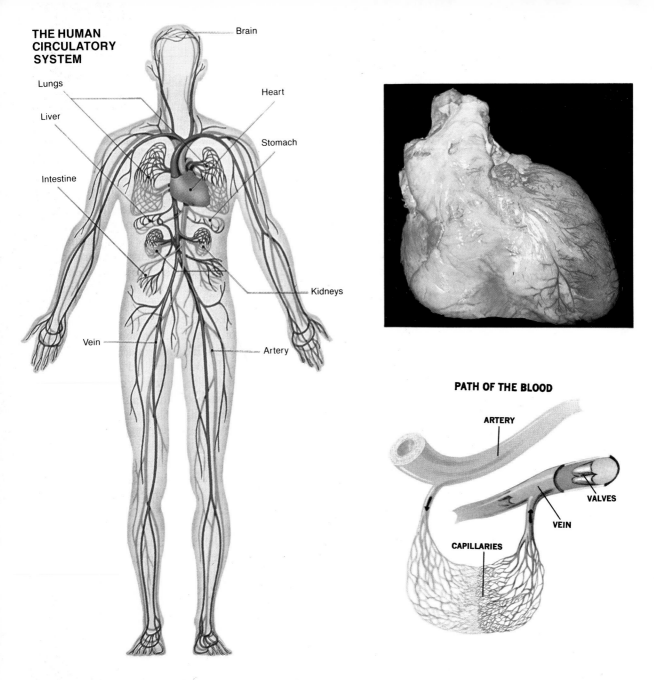

THE HUMAN CIRCULATORY SYSTEM

Brain

Lungs

Heart

Liver

Stomach

Intestine

Kidneys

Vein

Artery

PATH OF THE BLOOD

ARTERY

VALVES

VEIN

CAPILLARIES

The heart (above right) is a pump. It circulates blood throughout the body. The arteries (shown in red) carry blood to each organ and body part. Veins (shown in blue) carry blood away and return it to the heart.

also carry the waste product carbon dioxide from the various parts of the body back to the lungs. White blood cells fight infections and also provide the body with immunity to disease. Platelets are disk-shaped bodies that help form clots to stop bleeding.

Platelets and red and white cells are the blood's solid part. These solids are carried in the liquid portion, the plasma, which is made of

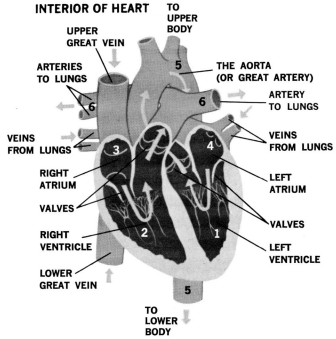

INTERIOR OF HEART

UPPER GREAT VEIN

TO UPPER BODY

ARTERIES TO LUNGS

5

THE AORTA (OR GREAT ARTERY)

6

6

ARTERY TO LUNGS

VEINS FROM LUNGS

VEINS FROM LUNGS

3

4

RIGHT ATRIUM

LEFT ATRIUM

VALVES

VALVES

RIGHT VENTRICLE

2

1

LEFT VENTRICLE

LOWER GREAT VEIN

5

TO LOWER BODY

water, proteins, and many other substances.

The blood is sent through the body by the other two elements of the circulatory system—the blood vessels and the heart. The body's millions of blood vessels range in size from microscopic vessels to ones thicker than a jump rope. There are three kinds of blood vessels—arteries, veins, and capillaries. Arteries carry blood from the heart to the rest of the body. Veins return blood from the body back to the heart. Visible only through a microscope, capillaries connect small arteries and veins to each other and also connect the circulatory system to other organs. The capillary walls are so thin that substances can go right through them back and forth between the circulatory system and the organs.

The heart, a muscle located near the middle of the chest, pumps the blood throughout the body. The adult heart weighs a little over half a pound and is about as big as a medium-sized apple, but it can do an amazing amount of work. Each minute your heart pumps about five quarts of blood, amounting to eighteen hundred gallons per day. In four weeks your heart pumps fifty thousand gallons of blood—enough to fill a good-sized swimming pool. However, your body does not make fifty thousand gallons of blood in those four weeks. Although new blood is constantly being created, the blood is

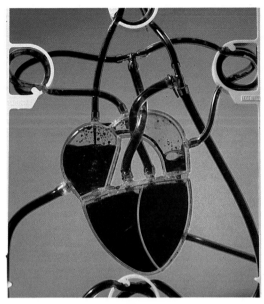

Blood flows into the upper chambers of the heart (left) when it is at rest. As the heart beats, the blood is pumped into the lower chambers (right) and then out to other parts of the body.

recirculated (used again and again) through the body.

Here is how the circulatory system works. First the heart pumps the blood through the arteries and into the millions of tiny capillaries in all areas of the body. The capillaries deliver the blood to all the body's cells. The blood feeds the cells oxygen and food and takes in carbon dioxide and other wastes produced by the cells. The blood transports the wastes to the heart through the veins. The heart sends these wastes to organs called the lungs that remove wastes from the blood.

In order to handle all the incoming blood at the same time that it pumps blood out to the body, the heart is divided into four chambers—two upper and two lower ones. The upper chambers, or atriums, collect the blood flowing into the heart. The lower chambers, called ventricles, pump the blood out of the heart.

Special muscles in the heart keep it pumping. These muscles cause the heart to contract (diminish in size) a little more than once per second. The contractions, felt as heartbeats, are what keep the blood moving through the heart. An adult's heart beats about seventy times a minute, while a child's beats about one hundred times per minute. When a person's body is under strain, the cells need more oxygen than usual. To deliver this extra oxygen, the heart beats more often than usual. That is why your heart speeds up when you are exercising, sick, or injured.

The Lymphatic System

Fluid containing water and other substances continually leaks from capillaries and nourishes body tissues. Most of the excess fluid that may be in the tissues seeps back into capillaries and returns to the bloodstream. The fluid that the capillaries cannot handle returns to the bloodstream through the lymphatic system.

Lymphatic vessels are located throughout the body and are similar to blood vessels. The excess fluid flows into the lymphatic vessels. This yellowish fluid, called *lymph*, empties back into the bloodstream near the heart.

Located at certain places along lymphatic vessels are some special round bodies called lymph nodes. The lymph nodes create white blood cells called lymphocytes. The lymphocytes, in turn, produce infection-fighting substances called antibodies. The lymph nodes also house large cells called *macrophages* that "eat up" foreign materials in the body. When germs and foreign substances carried by lymph pass through the lymph nodes, the antibodies and macrophages destroy them. The lymphocytes also make their way into the bloodstream and continue their work there.

A lymphocyte in the blood

The Respiratory System

All of the more than ten trillion cells in the body need oxygen. The body has a complex system for taking in and processing oxygen. It is called the respiratory system, and it includes the nose, mouth, pharynx, larynx, trachea, bronchial tubes, and lungs.

Respiration (breathing) begins when you pull in air. Breathing can be done through the nose *or* mouth because the nasal passage and throat join together into one tube called the pharynx behind the tongue. The air goes down the pharynx, down a tube called the larynx (voice box), and then down another tube called the trachea (windpipe). From the windpipe the air shoots down twin passages called the bronchi (one is a bronchus). Each bronchus passes into one of the two lungs, the main respiratory organs.

Inside each lung the bronchus branches off into smaller and smaller tubes, the littlest of which are called bronchioles. In turn, the bronchioles branch off into millions of tiny air sacs called alveoli. With the help of capillaries, the alveoli provide the body with oxygen and rid it of carbon dioxide.

Here is what happens in the lungs during respiration. The air that has been inhaled (breathed in) passes into the millions of alveoli. From the alveoli the air passes to the capillaries. Red blood cells in the capillaries then distribute the oxygen to all the cells in the body.

As the body cells use oxygen, carbon dioxide is formed as a waste product. The red cells in the bloodstream transport the carbon dioxide to the lungs. Once in the lungs, the carbon dioxide passes from the capillaries to the alveoli. The carbon dioxide is expelled from the alveoli when you exhale (breathe out).

A resting person takes about fourteen breaths per minute. During hard work the breathing rate increases, as is the case with the heart rate. An area of the brain's medulla oblongata called the respiratory center controls the breathing rate. The respiratory center monitors the amount of carbon dioxide in the bloodstream. When the carbon dioxide level is higher than normal, the respiratory center makes the breathing muscles work faster so that the excess carbon dioxide can

THE RESPIRATORY SYSTEM

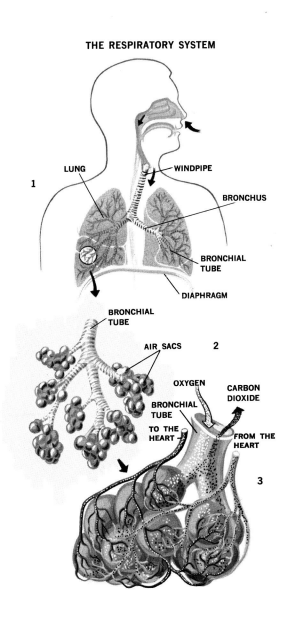

1

LUNG

WINDPIPE

BRONCHUS

BRONCHIAL TUBE

DIAPHRAGM

BRONCHIAL TUBE

AIR SACS

2

OXYGEN

CARBON DIOXIDE

BRONCHIAL TUBE

TO THE HEART

FROM THE HEART

3

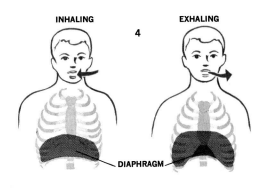

INHALING

EXHALING

4

DIAPHRAGM

NON-SMOKER

SMOKER

SMOKING DESTROYS LUNGS

Cigarette smoking damages the lungs and decreases their ability to expel carbon dioxide from the body and carry vital oxygen into the blood.

be expelled. Once the extra carbon dioxide has been exhaled, the respiratory center allows the breathing rate to return to normal.

The Digestive System

Every cell of your body needs food as well as oxygen. Since the cells are too small to be fed hot dogs, French fries, and other large foods directly, the body needs a way to break foods down into small pieces. The digestive system does this. The body parts involved in digestion include the mouth, teeth, salivary glands, pharynx, esophagus, stomach, small and large intestines, and the rectum. These are all part of a thirty-foot-long passage called the alimentary canal, or digestive canal.

Digestion starts in the mouth when your teeth chew your food. Young children have twenty primary teeth. At about age six the primary teeth begin to be replaced by the permanent teeth, which eventually number thirty-two.

As you chew, saliva is released onto your food by three pairs of salivary glands in your mouth and cheeks. Saliva softens the food and also contains enzymes (substances that speed up chemical processes) that help break the food down into simpler materials.

When you swallow, the food moves down into the pharynx behind the tongue. Part of the pharynx lets air as well as food pass through it. Since both food and air enter the pharynx, why doesn't food go down your breathing canal and wind up in your lungs instead of in your stomach? When you swallow, a little flap called the *epiglottis* suddenly folds over and covers the breathing passage like a lid. The epiglottis makes certain that food passing through the pharynx enters the digestive canal and not the breathing canal.

The swallowed food passes down from the pharynx into the muscular tube called the esophagus. Contractions of the esophagus move the food down into the stomach, the digestive canal's widest portion. The stomach produces an acid that helps kill germs in the food and enzymes that help digest it. The stomach also churns to make the food into a mush.

After the food has spent about three hours in the stomach the stomach muscles send it to the small intestine, a twenty-foot-long

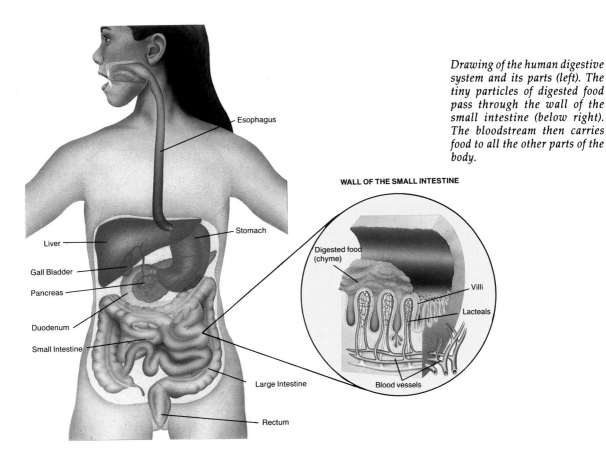

Drawing of the human digestive system and its parts (left). The tiny particles of digested food pass through the wall of the small intestine (below right). The bloodstream then carries food to all the other parts of the body.

Esophagus

Liver

Gall Bladder

Pancreas

Duodenum

Small Intestine

Stomach

Large Intestine

Rectum

WALL OF THE SMALL INTESTINE

Digested food (chyme)

Villi

Lacteals

Blood vessels

coiled tube. Inside the small intestine, enzymes complete the job of breaking the food down into simpler substances. Once these enzymes finish breaking down the food, digestion is completed.

Within the small intestine are millions of capillaries. Most of the digested food passes from the small intestine to the capillaries. Blood in the capillaries then carries it to the body cells. Lymphatic vessels carry the fatty foods from the small intestine to the bloodstream, which then distributes them to the body cells.

Some of the food in the small intestine cannot be used by the body. This waste material moves down to a five-foot-long tube called the *large intestine*. Inside the large intestine the water from the waste material is absorbed, leaving the wastes in solid form. The waste material (called *feces*) is expelled through a portion of the large intestine called the rectum and leaves the body through the opening called the anus.

The Urinary System

The blood contains some waste products besides carbon dioxide. If the body had no way to rid itself of these waste products in the blood, a person would eventually be poisoned. The job of removing these wastes from the bloodstream belongs to the urinary system, which is composed of the kidneys, ureters, bladder, and urethra.

The two kidneys are the main urinary organs. Blood flows into the kidneys through a big artery. Once inside the kidneys the blood is cleansed of its wastes by filtration units called nephrons. Each kidney has about a million nephrons, which separate the wastes from the usable portion of the blood.

The usable portion of the blood goes back to the heart through a big vein. The waste portion, called urine, travels from the kidneys through two tubes called ureters into a little storage tank called the bladder. From the bladder the urine leaves the body through a canal called the urethra. In males the urethra leads to the outside of the body through the penis. In females the urethra itself opens to the outside of the body.

When the bladder is full, sensory nerves in the bladder send a message up the spinal cord to the brain that it is time to urinate. The brain tells a special muscle to force urine out of the bladder. The average person produces about 1½ quarts of urine per day.

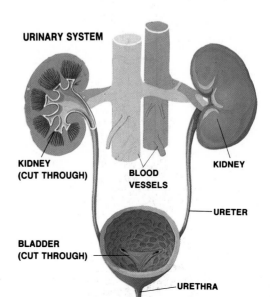

Diagram of the human urinary system.

The Glands

The dozens of organs that make and distribute chemicals needed by the body are called *glands*. There are two kinds of glands—endocrine and exocrine.

Endocrine glands. Endocrine glands discharge substances directly into the bloodstream. They include the adrenal glands, thyroid gland, pituitary gland, sex glands, and pancreas. The substances produced by the endocrine glands are chemical messengers called *hormones*.

Now and then there are reports of a person lifting a car off a pinned victim or doing another "superhuman" feat. These amazing displays of sudden strength are made possible by the two adrenal glands. Located atop the kidneys, the adrenal glands produce two hormones, adrenalin and noradrenalin, which help the body deal with emergencies. These hormones quicken and strengthen the heartbeat, widen the breathing passage to admit more air, and signal the liver to release extra sugar into the bloodstream for extra energy. The adrenal glands also perform several jobs during normal times, including regulating the use of food and the amount of salt in the body.

The *thyroid gland* lies next to the windpipe in the neck. This gland regulates metabolism—the rate at which food and oxygen are used by the body. Hormones produced by the thyroid also help control the development of the body and the brain.

Location of the major glands in the human body.

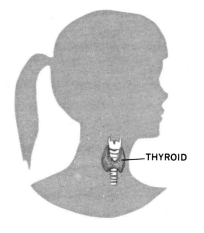

THYROID

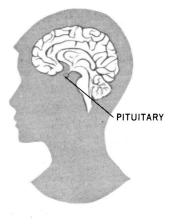

PITUITARY

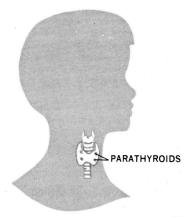

PARATHYROIDS

John Hollinden, a 7'5" basketball player, stands next to Patty Malone, a 3'2" actress.

The pituitary is called the "master gland" because it controls the activities of other endocrine glands. Located beneath the brain, the pea-sized pituitary releases hormones that stimulate the thyroid, adrenal, and sex glands. The pituitary gland also regulates growth. An underactive pituitary can cause dwarfism, a condition in which an adult may reach a height of just 4 feet or less. An overactive pituitary can cause gigantism, a condition in which a person may reach a height of 7½ feet or more.

The sex glands are the ovaries in females, and the testes in males. Hormones produced by the ovaries help females bear children. Hormones produced by the testes give males their deeper voices and hairy faces.

Exocrine glands. Unlike the endocrine glands that discharge substances directly into the blood, the exocrine glands release their products into the intestines or to the outside of the body. The exocrine glands include the liver, pancreas, sweat glands, tear glands, salivary glands, and mammary glands.

On the right side of the abdomen is the liver, the largest gland and one of the body's most vital organs. A person could not live for more than a few hours without this 3½-pound gland. The liver has many functions. A fluid called bile produced by the liver flows to the small intestine where it aids in digestion. The liver gathers waste products built up in the blood during digestion and converts them to urea, which later leaves the body in the urine. The liver stores a substance called glycogen that it sends to the body in sugar form when energy is required. The liver also stores vitamins and minerals that it releases when those substances are needed.

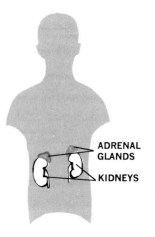

ADRENAL GLANDS

KIDNEYS

Another important organ, the pancreas, has aspects of both an endocrine and exocrine gland. The pancreas is considered an endocrine gland because it produces hormones, including insulin, that regulate the amount of sugar in the bloodstream. The pancreas is considered an exocrine gland because it releases juice that aids in digestion into the small intestine.

When you are hot or nervous, your skin and blood inform your brain about it. Your brain sends a message to the two million sweat glands located in the skin. The sweat glands air-condition the body by releasing perspiration (sweat) through their openings onto the skin. Sweat glands are largest and most numerous in such areas as the armpits, palms of the hands, soles of the feet, and forehead, causing those regions to sweat the most.

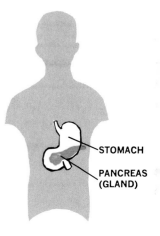

STOMACH

PANCREAS (GLAND)

Each time you blink, a tear gland behind each upper eyelid releases a small amount of fluid. This fluid provides the eyes with the moisture they need and also keeps the eyes clean. The tear glands are activated by special eye muscles. When you are sad, laughing hard, or have something in your eye, these muscles tighten. This squeezes out a few tears, which is why you cry.

When you eat, six major and many minor salivary glands in your mouth and cheeks release saliva. This is a liquid that softens the starchy food and begins breaking it down into simpler substances.

Mammals also have special exocrine glands called mammary glands on their chests. The mammary glands are undeveloped in males, but well-developed and important in females. As soon as a female gives birth, hormones stimulate the mammary glands to produce milk to feed the newborn. The milk leaves the mother's mammary glands through openings called nipples.

The Reproductive System

Each of us, like all other living creatures, must one day die. However, thanks to our reproductive systems, our human species can continue even though individuals pass out of existence. The reproductive system is the one area of the body in which males and females greatly differ. The reproductive organs are called genitals, or sex organs.

The male genitals include the penis, the scrotum, and the testes. The penis is a tube-shaped organ located in a male's groin. Behind the penis is the scrotum, a small pouch that contains the two round sex organs called testes. When a male is about thirteen-and-a-half years old, his testes start producing millions of sex cells called *spermatazoa*, or sperm.

The female genitals include the vagina, the uterus, and the ovaries. The vagina is a canal located in a female's groin. The vagina leads into the uterus, a pyramid-shaped, hollow organ. Two oval sex organs called ovaries lie not far from the uterus. Thin passages called oviducts lead from just outside the ovaries to the uterus.

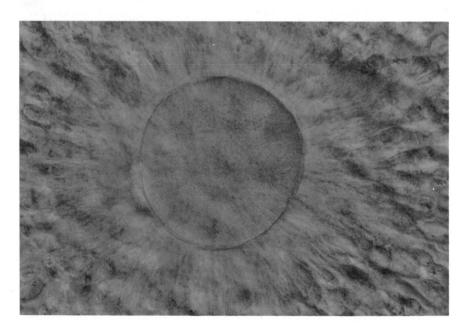

An unfertilized human egg

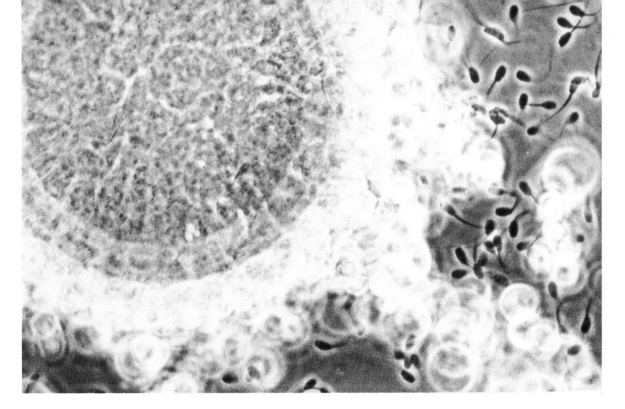

Photgraph of a human egg surrounded by sperm

When a female is about thirteen years old, her ovaries start producing eggs, one of which is released about every twenty-eight days in a process called ovulation. If the egg is not fertilized, it travels down one of the oviducts, goes down through the uterus, and exits the body (with some unneeded blood and tissue from the uterus) through the vagina. This process is called menstruation.

Everything works differently if the egg *is* fertilized. In order for that to happen, the male places his penis inside the female's vagina. Millions of sperm are discharged from the penis into the vagina. If one of the sperm unites with the egg in the oviduct, fertilization occurs. The fertilized egg then attaches itself to the uterus's lining, where it starts growing into a human being.

At first the fertilized egg is called an embryo, but at two months of age it becomes a fetus. At three months the fetus looks quite human, and at four or five months its heartbeat can be heard. After about nine months the fetus is ready to leave its mother's body. Uterine muscles force the baby out of the uterus, through the mother's vagina, and out into the world!

Chapter 8
How and Why Things Go Wrong

Each [disease] has its own nature, and each disease has a natural cause—and without a natural cause none arise.

Hippocrates

With its trillions of cells, hundreds of bones, dozens of organs, and several vital liquids such as blood and lymph, the human body is bound to have problems sometimes. There are hundreds of diseases—some caused by microbes, others by the wearing out of body parts, and still others by additional factors.

Diseases Caused by Microbes

Although invisible to the naked eye, microbes are all around us. They are in the air, in the ground, in oceans and lakes, and inside our bodies even when we are healthy.

Bacteria (one of which is called a bacterium) are among the most common microbes. Some bacteria, including ones in the intestines that aid in digestion, are helpful. Many others cause disease.

Bacteria are so small that many millions of them could fit into a teaspoon. Yet they are big compared to viruses, which also cause numerous diseases and which are the smallest known microbes. Viruses for the most part can only be seen with extremely powerful instruments called electron microscopes.

Scientists disagree on how to classify bacteria and viruses. Some say that bacteria are plants, while others think that, although alive, bacteria are neither plants nor animals. Viruses are so simple that scientists do not agree as to whether they are living or nonliving. Other microbes that can cause disease include molds, yeasts, and protozoans. Molds and yeasts belong to a large group of very simple plants called fungi, while protozoans are one-celled animals.

Scientists refer to disease-causing microbes as *pathogens*, but

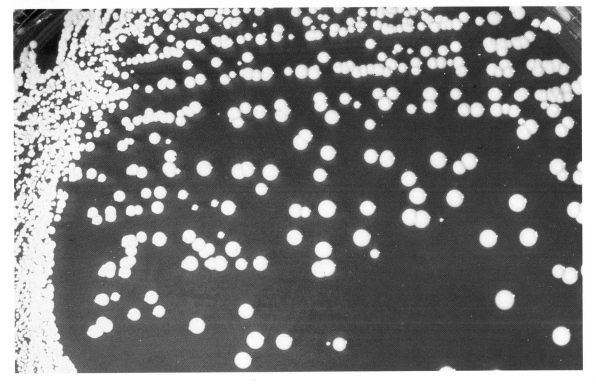

Staph bacteria (above) may cause painful skin infections.

most people call them germs. Once they have established them-selves inside the body, germs take control of the cells and tissues like creatures in a science-fiction story. They interrupt the normal func-tions of the cells and tissues, and this makes the victim sick. For ex-ample, common cold germs take control of the mucous membranes of the nose and throat, preventing a person from breathing and swallowing properly.

Most diseases caused by microbes are communicable. This means they can be spread from one individual to others. For example, in-fected people spread the common cold by sneezing and coughing. The cold viruses are also picked up by the hands of another person from a handshake or by touching a contaminated object. The vi-ruses are then passed by the hands to the nose or eyes where the in-fection starts. Syphilis and gonorrhea are venereal diseases—they are transmitted by sexual contact. Malaria victims are bitten by *Anopheles* mosquitoes that are infected by *Plasmodia* protozoans.

If we became ill every time we came near a sick person, life would be one long illness. Several factors determine whether a person will get sick after exposure to a certain germ. General physical condition

SOME DISEASES CAUSED BY MICROBES

Disease	Cause
African sleeping sickness	protozoans transmitted by tsetse flies
AIDS (Acquired Immune Deficiency Syndrome)	a virus
amebic dysentery	an amoeba
athlete's foot	a fungus
chicken pox	chicken pox virus
cholera	a bacterium
common cold	more than one hundred kinds of viruses
diphtheria	a bacterium
German measles	German measles virus
gonorrhea	a bacterium
hepatitis (viral)	at least two kinds of viruses
influenza	influenza viruses
leprosy	a bacterium
malaria	protozoans spread by *Anopheles* mosquitoes
measles	measles virus
mononucleosis	Epstein-Barr virus
multiple sclerosis	cause unknown
mumps	mumps virus
pneumonia (bacterial)	many different bacteria
pneumonia (viral)	many different viruses
polio	three kinds of viruses
rabies	rabies virus
rheumatic fever	streptococci bacteria
scarlet fever	streptococci bacteria
strep throat	streptococci bacteria
syphilis	a bacterium
tetanus	tetanus bacillus bacterium
tuberculosis	tubercle bacillus bacterium
typhoid fever	a bacterium
typhus	a rickettsia (type of microbe resembling small bacteria) that is transmitted by body lice and fleas
whooping cough	a bacterium
yellow fever	yellow fever virus, usually carried by *Aëdes aegypti* mosquitoes

and personal habits are important. Someone who doesn't eat a balanced diet, doesn't sleep enough, and smokes cigarettes may be more prone to disease than is a person with healthy habits. Also, someone who is already weak from illness is vulnerable to more serious diseases. Immunity is crucial, too. For many unknown reasons (including age and genetics), some people have poor immune systems, making them a target for a wide variety of diseases.

Geography and climate also figure in the occurrence of disease. Some germs—including those causing leprosy, yellow fever, and malaria—flourish in warm climates. People who live in places with cold climates are less likely to encounter these germs than those who live in tropical regions.

Degenerative Diseases

There are many diseases, called *degenerative diseases*, that gradually wear out the body. These diseases can strike at any time, but they are more common among the elderly. Degenerative diseases include heart and other cardiovascular problems, cancer, and arthritis.

Cardiovascular diseases. The term *cardio* comes from Greek and refers to the heart; *vascular* comes from Latin and refers to the blood vessels. Thus, cardiovascular diseases are ones affecting the heart and the blood vessels. Just as mechanical pumps and pipes wear out with age, cardiovascular problems occur much more often in older people than in young people.

One common cardiovascular problem is atherosclerosis, also known as arteriosclerosis—a disease in which arteries harden, thicken, and become blocked up by fatty substances. Fatty diet, high blood pressure, lack of exercise, cigarette smoking, and heredity (family traits) all can lead to arteriosclerosis. In turn, atherosclerosis can cause more serious problems, especially heart attacks and strokes.

As a person's arteries are increasingly clogged by fatty substances, the time can come when one of the coronary arteries (ves-

As the human body ages, it is more prone to heart attacks and strokes.

sels supplying the heart with blood) is almost totally blocked. When narrowed like that, a coronary artery tends to become so irritated that it forms a thrombus—a blood clot that finishes the job of blocking the artery. Once the heart is completely deprived of blood, a heart attack occurs. During an attack the heart may beat irregularly, stop beating completely, or suffer damage—all of which can result in death.

A stroke is similar to a heart attack, only in this case the artery blocked by fatty deposits and a blood clot is one supplying blood to the brain. Massive strokes often kill their victims. Those who survive a stroke are often left with brain damage resulting in paralysis and the inability to speak. As the main cause of heart attacks and of strokes, atherosclerosis is a very dangerous cardiovascular disease.

Also common is hypertension, or high blood pressure. Blood pressure is the force with which blood pushes against artery walls as it moves from the heart through the body. High blood pressure means that too much force is exerted on the arteries. This may cause damage to the arteries and other organs. By placing stress on the cardiovascular system, high blood pressure sets the stage for heart attacks and strokes.

In the United States heart attacks and other cardiovascular problems kill more than a million people per year—about as many as die from *all* other causes combined. Cardiovascular disease is also the leading cause of death worldwide.

Cancer. Several billion of the body's ten trillion cells die each minute. Normal cells are programmed to divide at a rate that keeps pace with the death of old ones. In the healthy body several billion new cells are produced each minute, keeping the total number of cells nearly constant.

It sometimes happens that a person's cells divide too quickly, and too many cells are produced. The out-of-control cells build up a mass of extra tissue in an organ. The disease in which cells run wild is called cancer, and the extra tissue is called a tumor.

Some tumors are for the most part harmless and are called benign tumors. Cells in a benign tumor do not differ greatly from normal cells, and the tumor itself is surrounded by a capsule. Benign tumors neither destroy the organs where they originate nor spread throughout the body. When a person's tumor is found to be benign, he or she does not have cancer.

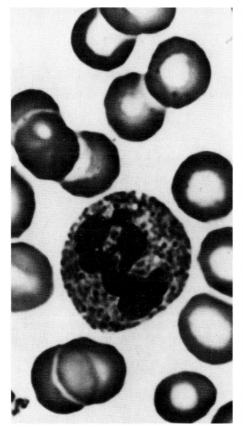 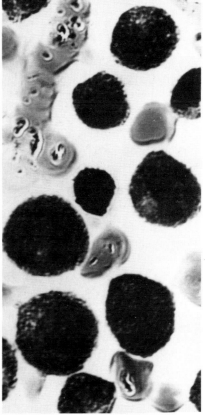

Notice the difference between the normal human blood cells (left) and leukemia-diseased blood cells (right).

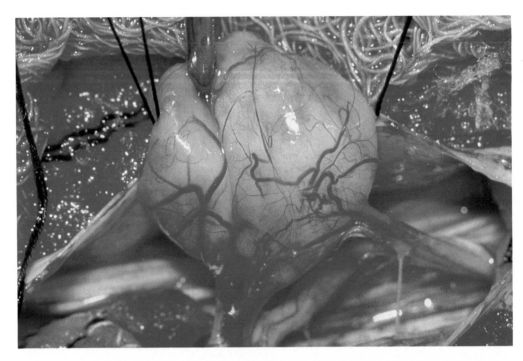

Tumor growing on the spinal cord

Other tumors are extremely harmful and are called malignant tumors. Cells in a malignant tumor multiply in a completely disorderly way and differ greatly from normal cells. Because they have no surrounding capsule, malignant tumors can badly damage an organ and also spread to other parts of the body. When a person's tumor is proved to be malignant, he or she does have cancer.

Cancer can develop in almost any organ of the body, but the most common places are the skin, digestive organs, female breasts, blood-forming organs, lungs, lymphatic organs, and the reproductive and urinary systems. Although cancer strikes people of all ages, it is much more common among elderly and middle-aged individuals and rare among children. Unless the cancer is removed early by surgery or destroyed by another method, the cancer cells can spread throughout the body by means of the blood and the lymph. The spread of cancer from the first site to new ones is called *metastasis*. Once the cancer strikes a vital organ, such as the liver, the patient will probably die.

Cancer-causing substances are called *carcinogens*. Many carcinogens have been identified. Cigarettes, for example, contain numerous carcinogens, which is why they cause most lung tumors. Certain kinds of radiation are also carcinogenic. Too much exposure to the sun's ultraviolet rays, for instance, causes most skin cancers. Asbestos and certain dyes and oil products can also cause cancer. Yet the causes of most cancers and the mechanisms by which cancer takes root in the cells remain unknown.

Cancer is a leading cause of death in most countries. In the United States where about half a million people died of cancer in 1985, it is the second leading cause of death, behind only cardiovascular disease.

CIGARETTE CARCINOGENS AND OTHER CHEMICALS

Some of the 2000 chemicals in cigarette smoke. Asterisks (*) mark proved carcinogens.

Acetaldehyde	Dibenzo[*a,e*]	Methylcarbazole
Acetone	fluoranthene*	5-Methylchry-
Acetylene	Dibenz[*a,b*]acri-	sene*
Acrolein	dine*	Methylfluoranthene*
Aminostilbene*	Dibenz[*a,j*]acri-	Methylindole
Ammonia	dine*	β-Naphthylamine*
Arsenic*	Dibenzo[*c,g*]	Nickel compounds*
Benz[*a*]anthracene*	carbazone*	Nicotine
Benz[*a*]pyrene*	*N*-Dibutylnitrosa-	Nitric oxide
Benzene*	mine*	Nitrobenzene
Benzo[*b*]fluoran-	Dichlorostilbene	Nitroethane
thene*	2,3-Dimethylchry-	Nitromethane
Benzo[*c*]phenan-	sene*	*N*-Nitrosodimethylamine*
threne*	Dimethylphenol	*N*-Nitrosomethylethyl-
Benzo[*j*]fluoran-	Ethane	amine*
thene	Ethanol	*N*-Nitrosodiethylamine*
Cadmium*	Ethylphenol	Nitrosonornicotine*
Carbazole	Fluoranthene	*N*-Nitrosonanabasine*
Carbon dioxide	Fluorene	*N*-Nitrosopiperidine*
Carbon monoxide	Formaldehyde	*N*-Nitrosopyrrolidine*
Chrysene*	Hexane	Phenol
Cresols	Hydrazine	Polonium-210*
Crotonaldehyde	Indeno[1,2,3-*cd*]	Propene
Cyanide	pyrene*	Pyridine
DDT	Indole	Sulfur dioxide
Dibenz[*a,c*]	Isoprene	Toluene
anthracene*	Methane	Vinyl acetate
	Methanol	

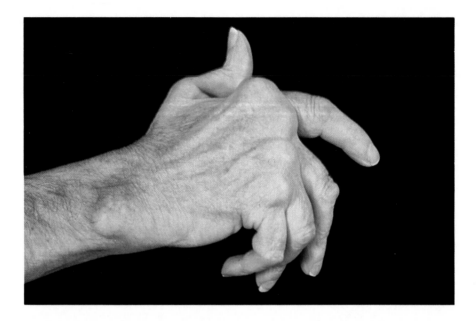

Close-up of a hand crippled by rheumatoid arthritis

Arthritis. Although far less serious than cancer, arthritis is much more common. More than forty million people—about one person out of every six in the United States—suffer from arthritis. Arthritis is also common in other nations where people live long lives.

Arthritis is a general term to describe diseases involving stiffness, pain, and swelling of the joints—places where bones meet. The most common form of arthritis is osteoarthritis. In this disease, cartilage (flexible tissue in the joints that normally keeps bones from rubbing against each other) wears out because of injury or many years of use. With the cartilage gone, the bones rub directly against one another, causing great pain. When elderly people complain about arthritis in their knees, hands, or hips, they usually mean osteoarthritis, which afflicts more than eighty percent of Americans sixty years and older.

More serious is rheumatoid arthritis, a disease in which the tissues in the joints thicken, and the inflamed tissue eats through the cartilage and the bone. The joints of rheumatoid arthritis patients often stiffen in abnormal positions. Without treatment, it can leave victims crippled. Rheumatoid arthritis usually first strikes adults between ages twenty and forty. Its cause or causes are unknown.

Gout is another arthritis disease involving painfully swollen joints. Occurring mainly among older men, gout is caused by a buildup of uric acid (a body chemical that normally leaves the body in the urine and the feces) in the blood. The high levels of uric acid form pain-producing crystals inside joints.

Alzheimer's disease. Alzheimer's is a degenerative disease in which the brain cells are gradually destroyed. In the early stages Alzheimer's patients (mostly elderly people) suffer memory loss. As more and more brain cells are destroyed, the victims eventually cannot care for themselves. Alzheimer's affects three million Americans and kills 120,000 of them yearly, making it a leading cause of death among the elderly. Its causes have yet to be identified.

FIVE OTHER DEGENERATIVE DISEASES

cirrhosis: a disease in which the liver is injured and scarred, causing reduced function of that vital organ

emphysema: an ailment (affecting mainly smokers) involving damage to the lungs' air sacs, causing difficult breathing

nephritis: a disease of the kidneys that can lead to kidney failure and uremia, a condition in which poisonous wastes accumulate in the blood

osteoporosis: a disease in which bones become porous (filled with holes) and brittle

peptic ulcers: open sores of the digestive system

Hormonal Diseases

Problems sometimes arise with the endocrine glands, the organs that produce the chemical messengers called hormones. The most common hormonal disease is diabetes mellitus, usually called diabetes. There are two kinds of diabetes, each involving a problem with insulin. Produced by the pancreas, insulin is the main hormone that regulates the body's use of sugar. Insulin helps carry sugar from the blood to the body cells for energy. In a diabetic's body, however, because of the insulin problem, the body cells cannot take in sugar, and there is an accumulation of too much sugar in the blood.

The milder and more common form of the disease is called *maturity-onset diabetes*; it is also known as *insulin-independent diabetes* or *Type II diabetes.* The pancreas of a maturity-onset diabetic produces enough insulin, but for reasons not yet understood the victim's body does not properly use the insulin. As a result, too much sugar builds up in the blood. Although the victim usually has no symptoms, sometimes he or she suffers from thirst, hunger, frequent urination, and weakness. Maturity-onset diabetics are usually middle-aged or elderly people who can control the disease through proper diet and weight control; sometimes medication is also used.

The less common but more serious form of diabetes is called *juvenile diabetes*; it is also known as *insulin-dependent diabetes* or *Type I diabetes.* The pancreas of a juvenile diabetic does not produce enough insulin. The result (if untreated) can be a very rapid buildup of sugar in the blood, causing similar but much stronger symptoms than those of maturity-onset diabetes. Although it can strike people of any age, juvenile diabetes tends to first appear between infancy and age forty. Juvenile diabetics must take insulin injections daily to stay alive.

Untreated, both juvenile and maturity-onset diabetes can lead to kidney disease, blindness, heart disease, peripheral vascular disease (blood vessel disease outside of the heart and its vessels), and stroke. In the United States, where twelve million people suffer from diabe-

Many diabetics must receive a daily injection (far right) of the insulin humulin (left).

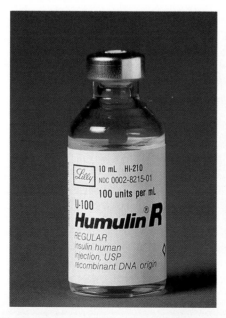
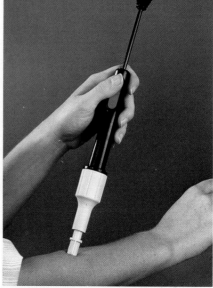

tes, the disease contributes to more than 100,000 deaths per year.

Other hormonal diseases include disorders of the thyroid, the gland that regulates metabolism or energy production. Persons with a severely underactive thyroid lose physical strength and tire easily because thyroid hormones are involved in chemical processes in almost every part of the body. Those with an overactive thyroid suffer from nervousness and rapid heartbeat because the gland has turned up their metabolism too high. Addison's disease, an ailment of the adrenal glands that causes weakness, fainting, and a tanned skin even on unexposed areas, is another hormonal disease.

Nutritional Diseases

Poor diet and a lack of food cause *nutritional diseases*. These are especially tragic if their victims are growing children.

Many nutritional diseases result from a lack of a particular vitamin. For example, lack of vitamin C can bring on scurvy, described earlier. Lack of vitamin D can bring on rickets, a disease that bends the bones into abnormal shapes. Vitamin deficiency diseases can usually be cured if the victims are given the missing vitamins.

Worldwide, the most common nutritional disease is malnutrition —a general lack of nourishing food, usually due to poverty. Malnu-

Millions of people die from malnutrition every year.

THE VITAMINS

Vitamin	Why Needed	Sources
A	For healthy eyes, skin, and urinary and respiratory systems	Milk, liver, sweet potatoes, carrots, butter, and yellow vegetables
B_1	For metabolism and for the heart and nervous systems	Yeast, whole-grain and enriched breads and cereals, meat, nuts, and most vegetables
B_2	For healthy skin, repair of tissue, and use of oxygen in the cells	Milk, eggs, cheese, liver, poultry, meat, fish, and green vegetables
Niacin	For healthy skin, nervous system, digestive tract	Milk, eggs, liver, meat, and whole-grain and enriched breads and cereals
B_6	For healthy teeth and gums, blood vessels, red blood cells, and nervous system	Whole-grain cereals, yeast, nuts, beans, meat, liver, fish, poultry, and most vegetables
Pantothenic Acid	For converting food into energy	Eggs, nuts, meat, and whole-grain cereals, liver, mushrooms
B_{12}	For red blood cells and nervous system	Eggs, meat, and milk and milk products, liver
Biotin	For circulatory system and skin	Eggs, nuts, liver, and most fresh vegetables
Folic Acid	For red blood cells	Leafy green vegetables, meat, mushrooms, liver, and yeast
C	For bones, teeth, wound healing, and metabolism	Citrus fruits, green vegetables, tomatoes, potatoes, raw cabbage, cantaloupe, and strawberries
D	For bone metabolism	Butter, fish, fish liver oils, eggs, liver, sunlight, tuna, salmon, and fortified milk
E	For cells	Whole-grain cereals and vegetable oils
K	For blood clotting	Leafy green vegetables, liver, cheese, butter

trition by itself usually does not cause death. However, malnutrition may weaken people to the point where they easily succumb to influenza, measles, pneumonia, and other diseases.

Although not many people in the United States and other developed countries die of the malnutrition-disease combination, worldwide more than fourteen million children die yearly from malnutrition and resulting diseases. Many of those who survive malnutrition grow up to be sickly adults.

Mental Illness

Most people have times when they are nervous, upset, or sad. Some people, however, are dominated by such problems. Those who are impaired by their own thoughts or feelings are suffering from mental illness, also called emotional illness. Mental illnesses are more difficult to identify than physical ones. Often, the difference between a "normal" and a mentally ill person is just a matter of degree. For example, it is normal to suffer from depression (prolonged sadness) after losing a job. However, someone who refuses to get out of bed after losing a job may be mentally ill, because that reaction seems too strong for the situation. The causes of a response also help define mental illness. For instance, it is normal to grieve after the death of a loved one. However, someone who mourns the loss of a favorite pencil is mentally ill, because a pencil doesn't merit such a response.

Depression is one of the most common of the many mental illnesses. Also common are anxiety disorders, which involve extremely strong fears about the future, and phobias, which involve strong fears of certain objects or situations. A common phobia is claustrophobia, the fear of being trapped in a closed place.

Victims of obsessive-compulsive disorders cannot help thinking the same thought, or repeating the same act (such as tying and untying their shoes or washing their hands) over and over. Those with manic-depressive disorders suffer mood swings ranging from over-excitement to extreme depression. Victims of the severe disease schizophrenia (Greek meaning "a split mind") withdraw from reality into a fantasy world. Persons who display paranoia imagine that others are out to "get" them in some way. In many cases, mentally ill people suffer from several disorders at the same time.

Children are special targets of several mental illnesses. Hyperactivity, a disorder whose victims cannot sit still or concentrate for long, is often outgrown by adulthood. On the other hand, autism, a disorder in which people have little or no capacity to talk or commu-

nicate, can be a lifelong condition. Its cause is unknown.

Little is known about the causes of mental illness. Hyperactivity and autism are thought to be inborn brain disorders, but scientists do not know how and why these conditions occur. Schizophrenic and manic-depressive people are thought to have chemical imbalances in their brains, but again few specific facts are known. Upsetting experiences can also trigger mental illness, but why some people cope with these experiences while others do not remains a mystery.

Mental illness is extremely common. The United States National Institute of Mental Health estimates that nearly one-fifth of all American adults are disabled at least somewhat by mental problems. These range from mild problems, such as a fear of riding in elevators, to severe ones such as extreme paranoia. Some mentally ill people become so unhappy that they kill themselves. In the United States, about thirty thousand people per year commit suicide.

Accidents

People can be perfectly healthy one instant and badly in need of medical care the next instant because of an accident.

One of the most common accidents is the fracture, or broken bone. In a simple fracture a bone breaks, but the skin remains unbroken. More serious is a compound fracture, in which bone fragments actually protrude through the skin. In a multiple fracture the bone is broken in more than one place.

Bruises, caused by blows to the body, can also be very painful and damaging. A head bruise can cause concussion, an injury to the brain that can result in unconsciousness and memory loss.

Burns and scalds are other common types of accidental injuries. Caused by fire, electricity, or chemicals, burns can damage or even destroy the skin. Injuries from hot liquids or steam are called scalds and do the same kinds of harm as burns.

Poisoning is another kind of accident. Food poisoning comes from eating food infected by harmful bacteria or by other harmful substances. Chemicals and fumes, bee and wasp stings, and the bites of certain snakes and spiders can also cause poisoning. If a poison affects a vital process such as breathing or heart or liver function, the victim can die.

Accidents claim many more lives than most people realize. In the United States, 100,000 accident victims die each year, making accidents one of the country's leading causes of death.

MAIN TYPES OF ACCIDENTAL DEATHS IN THE UNITED STATES (1984)	
Type of Accident	Number of Deaths
Motor Vehicle	46,200
Falls	11,600
Fires	10,000
Drowning	5,700
Poisoning	5,200
Choking on Food or Other Objects	3,100
Accidental Shootings	1,800

Chapter 9
Modern Medicine Strikes Back!

The physician's business is to know the different kinds of disease, to understand their causes and symptoms, furthermore to prescribe remedies with discernment and perseverance and according to the special circumstances to help everyone as much as possible. . . .

Paracelsus

If Hippocrates could visit a modern doctor's office or hospital, he would probably be amazed by all the medicines and machines used by today's physicians. Yet he would find that medicine's goals have not changed in the twenty-four centuries since he said that doctors should work "for the benefit of the sick."

Doctors

Because they diagnose diseases and decide how to treat them, doctors are among the most important people in the medical world. Doctors receive more education than is required by many other professions. In the United States, a man or woman wanting to become a doctor must first complete a regular college program and then attend medical school for four more years. Medical school graduates receive a Doctor of Medicine degree, usually called an M.D.

To gain experience, most new doctors in the United States serve for at least a year as interns in a hospital, where they work long hours under experienced doctors. After that, the young doctors become hospital residents; during their residencies, they work in the field of medicine in which they will practice when they set up their own offices. Following two to four years of residency, some doctors take a two-year fellowship in a specialized field. In addition, before they can practice medicine on their own, doctors in the United States and most other countries must pass a licensing test.

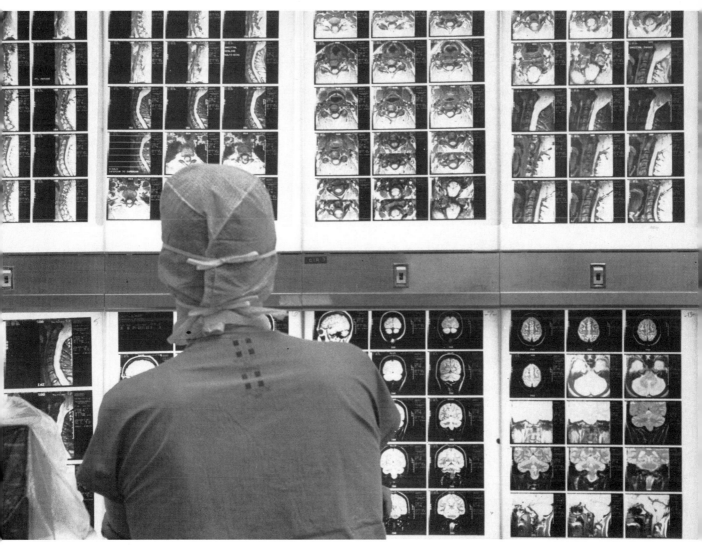

Doctors who become general practitioners or family doctors provide a variety of basic health care, from delivering babies to setting broken bones. Doctors who become experts in a particular field are called specialists. In the poor nations people desperately need a variety of health care, and so the few doctors there tend to be general practitioners. Specialization is more common in the wealthier nations where there is an adequate supply of doctors. In the United States, 80 percent of the 350,000 doctors are specialists.

A neurosurgeon studies brain and spinal cord scans at the Chicago NeuroSurgical Center in Columbus Hospital.

Twenty-five Kinds of Medical Specialists

allergists—doctors who are allergy experts

anesthesiologists—doctors who administer anesthesia during operations

cardiologists—doctors who are experts on the heart

dermatologists—doctors who are experts on skin disorders

endocrinologists—doctors who are experts on the endocrine glands

epidemiologists—doctors who are experts on the occurrence of disease among large numbers of people

gastroenterologists—doctors who are experts on the stomach and digestive organs

general surgeons—doctors who perform operations not covered by other surgical specialists

gynecologists—doctors who treat diseases of the female reproductive system (gynecologists are usually also obstetricians who deliver babies) *hematologists—doctors who are experts on the blood and the blood-forming organs*

internists—doctors who are experts on internal organ problems

nephrologists—doctors who are experts on the kidneys

neurologists—doctors who are experts on the nervous system

obstetricians—doctors who deliver babies and who care for the mother before and after childbirth (obstetricians are usually also gynecologists who treat diseases of the female reproductive system)

oncologists—doctors who are experts on cancer

ophthalmologists—doctors who are experts on eye diseases

orthopedic surgeons—surgeons who operate on bones and on other parts of the skeletal system

otolaryngologists—doctors who are experts on ear, nose, and throat

pathologists—doctors who study the causes, symptoms, and effects of diseases

pediatricians—doctors who specialize in treating children

podiatrists—doctors who are experts on foot diseases

psychiatrists—doctors who are experts on mental illnesses

radiologists—doctors who use X rays and radioactive substances to diagnose diseases and treat patients

thoracic surgeons—surgeons who operate on the chest

urologists—doctors who treat the urinary tract and the male sex organs

Not all doctors treat patients. Some are medical researchers—men and women who work in laboratories to find better ways of dealing with health problems. For example, thousands of researchers around the world are working to find the ca ises and cures for cancer. Other doctors who do not treat patients work as professors

Doctor referring to a mammogram during consultation with a breast cancer patient

in universities where they train future doctors. Some doctors find time to treat patients, do research, and teach at a university.

Doctors who treat patients have offices where people come to be examined. Some of those who visit the doctor are already sick or injured, while others are there for checkups. Checkups are very important, because some diseases that are fatal in advanced stages can be cured when caught early.

During a checkup a doctor may ask questions to learn the patient's medical history, look at and press the patient's body to determine if anything is abnormal, take the patient's temperature, listen to the patient's heart and lungs with a stethoscope, measure his or her blood pressure, and take blood and urine samples. Usually more information can be obtained from the medical history and physical examination than from any other method. A doctor who wants to learn about something deep inside the patient may order an X ray or other tests. To prevent disease, especially among children, the doctor may give the patient one or more vaccinations during the checkup.

Hospitals

If a patient has something wrong, the doctor makes a diagnosis —a conclusion regarding the nature of the illness based on the person's history, physical exam, and tests. Patients needing operations or special care are usually sent to hospitals. Besides maintaining their own offices, many doctors are on hospital staffs. This allows them to supervise their patients who need hospitalization.

Hospitals have much more equipment than doctors can keep in their offices. Among these are X-ray machines, which provide pictures of patients' insides; linear accelerators, which bombard cancer cells with high-energy radiation; heart-lung machines, which serve as a patient's heart and lungs during heart surgery; incubators, which provide premature infants with heat and air; monitors, which keep track of a patient's blood pressure and heartbeat; and dialysis machines, which purify the blood for those whose kidneys cannot do the job. A large hospital will have dozens of other complex machines.

Magnetic Resonance Imaging scanner

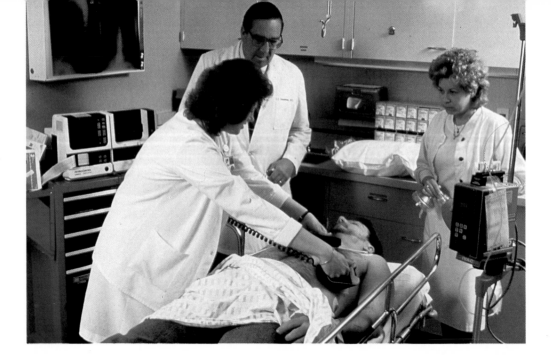

CPR being administered to a patient in an emergency room

Large hospitals are divided into units or wards, each providing a special kind of care. The emergency unit is equipped to handle unexpected health problems. Hospitalized children usually stay in the pediatric unit. Patients undergoing operations stay in the surgical unit, those with mental problems occupy the psychiatric unit, and those with tumors populate the cancer unit. A hospital's happiest section is always the maternity unit, where newborn babies and their mothers stay.

Although doctors decide the course of treatment, nurses keep hospitalized patients comfortable. Nurses bring patients their medicine, record temperatures and blood pressure results, and often explain the treatments to them. To become professional nurses, usually called registered nurses in the United States, women and men must attend nursing school for several years. Practical nurses have less training than registered nurses—usually about a year— and help the professional nurses with their work. Nurses' aides have less training than practical nurses and do much of the physical work, such as bathing patients.

Other hospital workers include pharmacists, who dispense the medicines prescribed by doctors; laboratory technologists, who perform lab tests; radiological technologists, who take the X rays

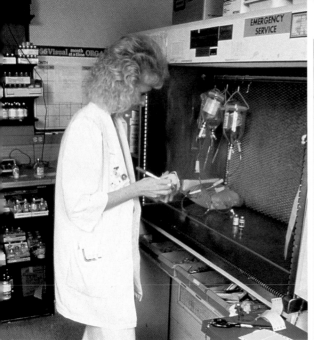

Left: Technician preparing IVs. Above: Patient consulting a dietitian

and give the X-ray treatments ordered by doctors; physical therapists, who help patients recover through exercise, special baths, and heating devices; and dieticians, who make sure that all patients get the foods they need.

Preventive Medicine

It is better to discover a disease in its early rather than in its later stages. However, it is even better to prevent the disease altogether. The methods used to help people avoid diseases are known as preventive medicine.

Vaccinations, also called inoculations, immunizations, or shots, have been a major tool of preventive medicine ever since Edward Jenner devised a smallpox vaccine in the late 1700s. Vaccinations introduce dead or harmless germs or parts of germs into people's bodies. This stimulates the white blood cells to produce substances called *antibodies* against particular diseases. If the person is later exposed to the actual disease, he or she already has the antibodies to fight it off.

Diseases for which vaccines have been made include diphtheria, tetanus, whooping cough, German measles, measles, mumps, polio, cholera, yellow fever, bubonic plague, influenza, rabies, hepatitis, and tuberculosis. Because of the slight risk of getting sick from a vaccination, people are not given every one in existence. Instead, doctors vaccinate people only against diseases that pose a real threat. For instance, children in the United States no longer receive the smallpox vaccine, because smallpox has been wiped out all over the world, but they are routinely vaccinated against diphtheria, tetanus, whooping cough, German measles, measles, mumps, and polio. Each year doctors in the United States give the influenza vaccine to the elderly and other high-risk patients.

Proper diet and exercise are two other key preventive medical measures. For example, people prone to heart disease are often placed on special diet and exercise programs to help them avoid problems. Those whose families suffer from diabetes or certain cancers are often told by their doctors to follow special diets, too.

The decision not to smoke cigarettes is one of the best preventive measures people can take for themselves. Lung cancer is now the deadliest form of cancer in the United States, claiming more than 125,000 lives per year. Most of those dead people were cigarette smokers. Cigarettes have also been linked to cancer of the mouth, pharynx, larynx, esophagus, stomach, pancreas, and bladder. In addition, cigarette smokers are more than twice as likely to have heart attacks as nonsmokers and are more prone to emphysema and stomach ulcers.

Drugs

Once people are sick, it is too late for preventive medicine. Sick people need to be cured, or at least be made to feel better. The substances doctors use to help the sick and injured are called drugs, or medicines. Today's doctors have many hundreds of drugs at their disposal, including ones to steady the heartbeat, strengthen the heartbeat, slow the spread of cancer, kill germs, dull pain, put patients to sleep for surgery, and provide substances that some people's bodies cannot make on their own.

Drugs come from many sources. Many antibiotics are made from fungi or by chemical means. The painkiller morphine and the heart medicine digitalis are two drugs made from plants. Animals provide other drugs, including the insulin taken from cattle and pigs that is used to treat human diabetics. Bacteria can also be used as "drug factories" in an interesting process called *recombinant DNA technology,* which will be described later. However, most drugs today are synthetic—that is, made out of chemicals in a laboratory. The sulfa drugs that fight bacterial infections and the tranquilizers that calm nervous people are among the synthetic drugs.

Most of the more than fifty cancer drugs now in use are also synthetic. The use of drugs to combat any disease is technically called chemotherapy, but the word is usually used mainly to describe cancer-fighting drug treatments. Chemotherapy has become quite successful in treating leukemia, a cancer in which the white blood cells reproduce in an uncontrolled manner.

Whatever their sources, all drugs work by the same principles. They alter the usual activities of cells, either killing them or changing them in some way. Antibiotics, for example, disrupt the cellular processes of bacteria so much that they die. Tranquilizers slow down cellular activity in the nervous system, which calms patients. Anesthetics slow the nervous system to the point where the patient loses consciousness.

All drugs can be harmful if incorrectly used. Even aspirin can be deadly if enough of them are taken. However, aspirin and other relatively safe drugs are sold over the counter in stores and are known as nonprescription drugs. More powerful drugs must be prescribed by a doctor and are called prescription drugs.

Large numbers of people—including millions in the United States—are drug abusers. Most of the abused drugs are illegal ones such as heroin, cocaine, and marijuana. Nevertheless, there are also many abusers of prescription or even over-the-counter drugs. For example, some people obtain sleeping pills and/or tranquilizers from several doctors. If they take too many of the pills, they can harm or even kill themselves.

Surgery

Some diseases, injuries, and deformities can only be cured by surgery (operations). Doctors who perform operations are called surgeons. Surgeons are M.D.'s like other doctors, but they have had specialized surgical training.

After entering the hospital, the surgical patient is examined to make sure that he or she can withstand the operation. Doctors also study the patient's medical history to be prepared for any unusual reaction that may occur during surgery. The anesthesiologist discusses various anesthetics with the patient to determine the safest and best one for this particular case. Before surgery, a sample of the patient's blood is also drawn so that the hospital can have the same type of blood ready if a transfusion is needed.

The surgery is performed in the "O.R." or operating room. Heading the surgical team are the surgeon and anesthesiologist. Also in the O.R. are several surgical nurses, who hand instruments to the surgeon and monitor the machines that record the patient's vital signs. The head surgeon may also have an assistant surgeon who helps in the operation.

Surgeons performing a liver transplant

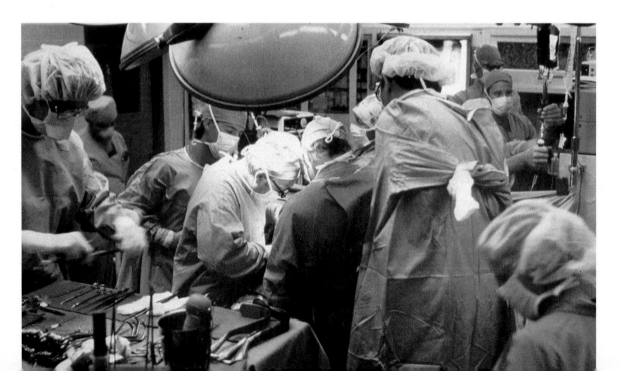

Operations can take from a few minutes to a few hours, depending on their complexity. During a long operation, the patient may need additional anesthesia, which the anesthesiologist provides. At the end of the operation the surgeon sews up the incision (opening) that was made to gain entry to the patient's insides. The threads used for this are called sutures, but most people call them *stitches*.

Cancer surgery. Of all those who get cancer, about 60 percent die of the disease within five years and the other 40 percent are "cured." "Cured" is placed in quotation marks because no one can guarantee that the cancer will not recur.

Surgery is by far the main way of curing cancer. Although some leukemias and lymphomas (cancers of the lymphatic system) are cured by chemotherapy and some tumors are shrunk by chemotherapy, X rays, and other methods, the surest way of destroying tumors is to cut them out.

The key to successful cancer surgery is finding the tumor early, before the cancer cells have spread. If the tumor is undetected too long, the cancer cells can metastasize (spread) through the blood or lymph to other organs. Once that happens, the patient may develop so many tumors that the case is hopeless.

Because cancer can spread through the lymph system, surgeons often remove nearby lymph glands while cutting out a tumor. They also usually remove tissue surrounding the tumor to be as sure as possible that no cancerous cells are left in the area.

Cardiovascular surgery. The coronary artery bypass, an operation that came into use in the late 1960s, is now so common that over 100,000 of them are done yearly in the United States. Bypasses are done on people whose coronary arteries are so blocked that they risk heart attacks or related problems. In a bypass, a piece of vein from the patient's leg or the internal mammary artery from the chest is attached to the coronary arteries in such a way that the blood can flow around the blockage, much as a car on the highway detours around a roadblock.

In the early 1980s a new method called *balloon angioplasty* came

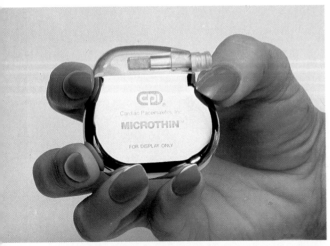

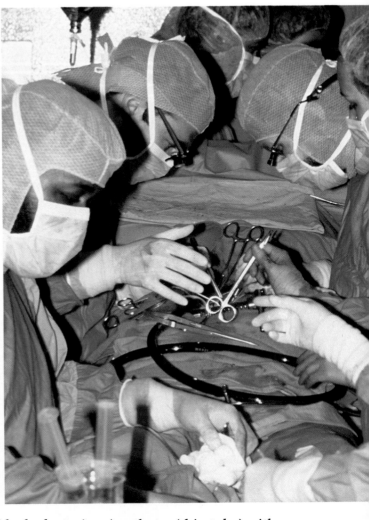

Right: Cardiovascular surgery. Top left: Human pacemaker. Above: Balloon catheter for angioplasty in a coronary artery

into use for clearing out blocked arteries. A catheter (thin tube) with a balloon attached to it is inserted into the clogged artery. As the balloon is inflated, the material blocking the artery is pushed away against the wall of the artery. Balloon angioplasty is much simpler surgery than the bypass, but it is not suitable for every patient. Laser treatment to clear clogged blood vessels may be the therapy of the future for blocked arteries.

"Blue babies" can also be helped with surgery. These babies, whose skin looks bluish from lack of oxygen, have a variety of abnormalities involving their hearts that prevent normal blood flow.

Surgeons can repair many of these abnormalities today, enabling many of the babies to live normal lives.

Heart valve operations are also common. A small percentage of babies are born with faulty heart valves, and some people develop bad valves later in life. This can result in heart failure. Heart surgeons can repair the faulty valves in some cases. In other cases they can replace the bad valves with artificial ones or with valves taken from pigs.

An irregular heartbeat is another problem that can result in sudden death. Cardiologists can place pacemakers in the chests of some patients with irregular heartbeats. A pacemaker is a battery-powered device that stimulates a more normal heart rhythm.

Surgery to correct defects. Congenital defects are ones present at birth. There are many congenital defects besides the defective heart valves just described. Spina bifida (meaning "open spine") is a congenital defect in which a baby's spinal cord protrudes through a gap in the bones in the back. Until recent years, this disorder was virtually untreatable, and many of its victims were left paralyzed. Today, surgeons can close up the spines of many spina bifida victims, avoiding this paralysis.

Most defects develop in the course of life. Several developmental heart defects have already been discussed. A much less serious problem is tonsillitis, an infection of the throat tissues called tonsils. If inflamed badly enough, the tonsils may be removed in an operation called a tonsillectomy. The appendix—a small, unneeded portion of the intestine—can also become badly inflamed and infected. In that case the appendix must be removed in an operation called an appendectomy.

Another common defect, abdominal hernia, occurs when part of the intestine pushes through the abdominal (stomach wall) muscles. Hernias are usually operated on before the intestine is trapped in the hernia and becomes badly twisted and inflamed. A twisted intestine can lead to strangulation in which the intestine is constricted in the stomach wall muscles and its blood supply is cut off.

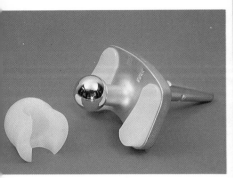

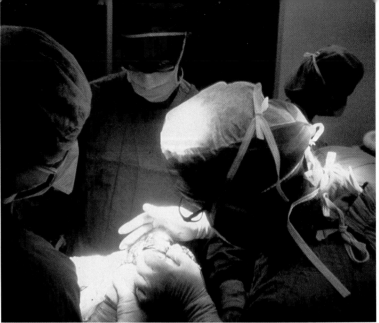

Right: Orthopedic surgeons implanting an artificial knee joint. Above: An artificial knee joint.

Sometimes, also in the course of life, people break bones, and need orthopedic surgeons to fix them. Orthopedic surgeons also operate on many other kinds of bone and joint problems.

Organ transplants. Up until a few years ago, transplantation of major organs often ended in failure because the body's immune system rejected the new organ. The introduction of the drug cyclosporine in the early 1980s helped ease the rejection problem. Surgical improvements and better organ preservation methods have also boosted the success rate for organ transplants.

There are four sources for organs that are used in transplants. The organs can come from the patient's own body, from animals, from another living person, or from a dead body.

Severely burned people needing skin grafts usually have good skin from their own bodies transplanted to the damaged area. The coronary artery bypass also uses materials from patients' own bodies. The transplantation of pigs' heart valves into humans is an example of the use of animal organs.

Because the human body has two kidneys and can function well with just one, some people with failing kidneys receive a transplant from a sister or brother. Some people needing bone marrow transplants because of leukemia or other diseases also receive the material from living donors, almost always a brother or sister. However, each of us has just one heart, liver, and pancreas. Donation of those organs as well as eyes comes from cadavers (dead bodies).

Aside from the scientific problems, organ transplantation still has two practical problems. Not enough organs are available, and the operations are very expensive. Doctors are now experimenting with artificial hearts and other organs, which may one day help solve these problems.

The Future Will Be Better

Just as we consider the medicine of the year 1900 rather primitive, the day will come when people will call our medicine of today primitive. They will be amazed that in the "old days" so many people died of heart attacks and cancer. They will be astounded that other diseases claimed so many lives and that so many poor people missed out on the benefits of medicine.

Thousands of researchers around the world are working to turn cancer, heart disease, and other medical problems into relics of the past, as was done with smallpox. To learn about their progress, the author (who from here on will call himself "I") spent more than a year visiting, phoning, and writing to about fifty medical researchers and doctors. In the next section, you will see how the work they are doing is shaping the medicine of tomorrow.

Laser eye surgery

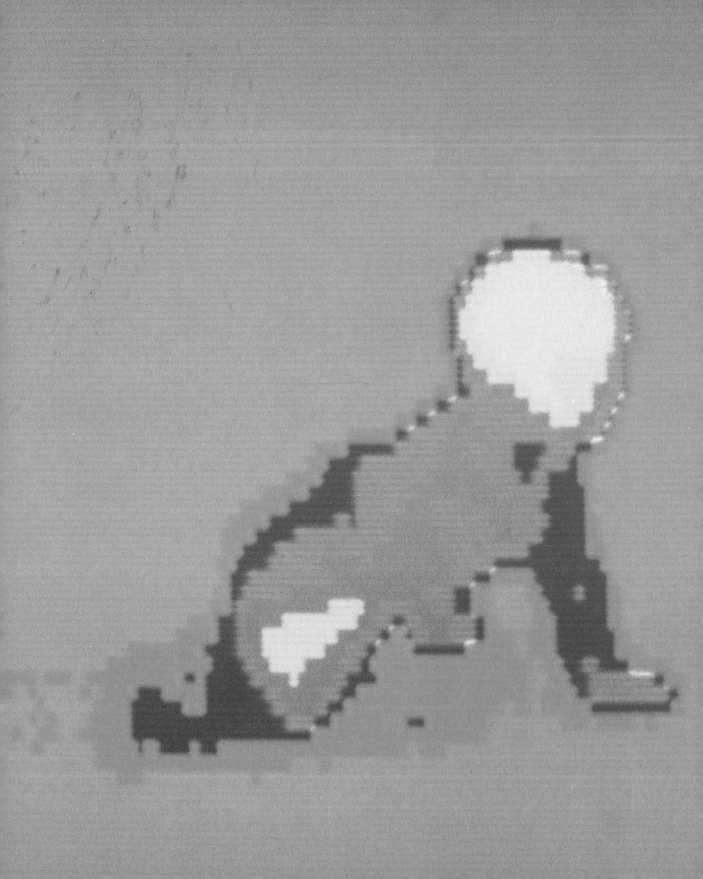

PART III: TOMORROW

Thermographic photo of an infant

Chapter 10
The War Against Cancer

They can send men to the Moon, but they couldn't do a damned thing about Mother's cancer.

The author's father, a few minutes after
the author's mother died of cancer

Someday we should be able to make cancer cells revert back into normal cells. That's going to happen, but before we can do it we have to understand the mechanisms by which cancer works.

Dr. Thomas Spelsberg, Department of
Biochemistry and Molecular Biology,
Mayo Clinic

A Terrible Killer

Cancer is one of the main killers of human beings. Because it generally does not appear until people are past sixty, cancer is more common in developed countries where people live longer than in poor ones where many die young. In the United States, where half a million people died of it in 1985, cancer is second only to heart disease as the leading cause of death. The most disturbing statistic is that cancer has steadily become more common in the United States ever since cancer statistics have been kept. The American Cancer Society, a research and educational organization, says that a child born in the United States in 1987 has more than one in three chances of one day developing cancer and better than one in five chances of dying of it. Many other countries have similar statistics.

The one ray of hope is that these predictions were based on what was known about combating cancer as of 1987. These statistics may be changed for the better by thousands of scientists who are working in five major areas of cancer research:

- *The causes of cancer*
- *The mechanisms of cancer*
- *The prevention of cancer*
- *Improved methods of diagnosis*
- *Improved methods of cancer treatment*

Learning More About the Causes of Cancer

In the early 1900s, lung cancer was so rare that many doctors had never seen it. During the 1930s lung cancer became more common, and during the 1960s it passed breast cancer as the number one cancer killer. Today lung cancer claims more than twice the lives per year as the second leading cancer killer: tumors of the colon (portion of the large intestine) and rectum.

Some doctors of the 1930s and 1940s suspected that cigarettes had caused the increase in lung cancer. Studies were made comparing lung cancer among smokers and nonsmokers. Again and again, lung cancer was shown to be much more common among smokers. Two factors had combined to create the lung cancer increase of the 1930s. First, cigarette smoking had suddenly become popular around 1915. Second, cigarette carcinogens usually take a couple of decades to create a tumor.

Lung cancer (left) is caused by exposure to cigarette smoke, lethal minerals and chemicals, and polluted air.

129

The proof linking cigarettes to lung cancer became so massive that in 1965 the United States Congress passed a law requiring tobacco companies to place health warnings on cigarette packages. Several years later, Congress banned cigarette ads on TV and radio. Thanks partly to these measures, between 1964 and 1986 the percentage of American adults who smoked dropped from 45 to 30 percent. Hopefully smoking will continue to lose popularity. Since cigarettes cause 85 percent of all lung cancer deaths, a big drop in smoking's popularity should eventually result in a big drop in the lung cancer rate.

Researchers generally follow a step-by-step process when linking a substance to cancer. First, someone suspects that a substance causes cancer. Next, scientists compare cancer statistics for people who have and have not been exposed to the substance. There may also be studies to see if the substance causes cancer in mice and other animals. These were the basic steps in finding out that cigarettes, the Sun's rays, asbestos, certain dyes and oil products, many potent chemicals, and nuclear radiation can cause cancer.

Currently researchers are zeroing in on differences in diet to see if they cause some of the cancer variations between countries. For example, it has long been known that the United States has a high colon cancer rate and a low stomach cancer rate. Japan, on the other hand, has a low colon cancer rate but a very high stomach cancer rate. Might dietary differences between the United States and Japan cause these variations in digestive system cancers?

Just as doctors suspected it before they could prove that cigarettes caused lung cancer, many doctors now think that the large amount of fat (particularly animal fat) in the American diet helps cause the country's high colon cancer rate. Japan's high stomach cancer rate may result from their overuse of salt and certain flavorings and from their charring of food during cooking. Proving all this is more difficult than proving the lung cancer-cigarette connection. One problem is determining the foods people have eaten during their entire lifetimes.

Dr. Roy E. Shore

Dr. Roy E. Shore of New York University Medical Center in New York City is a leading researcher of the cancer-fat connection. Between 1984 and 1986 Dr. Shore and his co-workers interviewed about eight hundred people in three New York City hospitals about their diets. About 350 of the interviewees were chosen because they had colon cancer, while the other 450 were in the hospital for noncancerous conditions.

"The idea is to compare diets, to see if we can tell which dietary factors promote or inhibit the development of colon cancer," explained Dr. Shore. "Fats are probably the single most likely cause of colon cancer," he *thinks*, and several other studies indicate that this is the case. However, like any good scientist, he will wait until all his facts are analyzed before making a conclusion.

Even if fats are definitely linked to colon cancer, we must be careful about changing our diets, explained Dr. Charles Moertel, Chairman of the Oncology Department at the Mayo Clinic in Rochester, Minnesota. The problem is that the foods we turn to may cause a different kind of cancer!

"True, we have more colon cancer and less stomach cancer than the Japanese," Dr. Moertel explained. "Some think that the Japanese have less colon cancer because they eat less fat and more fiber [fresh

Dr. Charles G. Moertel

fruits, vegetables, and whole-grain breads and cereals]. But don't forget that the Japanese have a very high incidence of stomach cancer. We can cure 50 percent of colon cancer but only about 10 percent of stomach cancer, so changing our diet for theirs may not be a good trade."

Dr. Moertel's comments underscored the fact that researchers have not been studying the relationship between diet and cancer for very long. Many more studies are needed (and some are now being done) to learn whether certain foods cause certain cancers. Hopefully we will one day know the ideal diet for avoiding as many kinds of cancer as possible.

The link between radiation and cancer also interests many researchers. To learn about work being done on this subject I drove twenty-five miles southwest of Chicago, Illinois, to Argonne National Laboratory, a science research center managed by the University of Chicago for the United States Department of Energy. There I visited with Dr. Tom Fritz, a veterinarian in the Biological and Medical Research Department.

Dr. Fritz explained that such forms of radiation as ultraviolet rays, gamma rays, X rays, and nuclear radiation are known to cause cancer. Nevertheless, several key questions about radiation remain.

How harmful is low-level radiation? How big a dose of various kinds of radiation does it take to produce cancer? Some researchers are trying to answer these and other questions by analyzing cancer statistics for people who work with various forms of radiation. Others, including Dr. Fritz, experiment on animals to see how radiation affects them.

"One current topic of interest is the effect of radiation from TV sets, microwave ovens, and other low-level sources in daily life," said Dr. Fritz. Several disturbing studies indicate that certain cancers may be caused by long-term exposure to common low-level radiation. However, some scientists feel that these studies are not conclusive and that exposure to low-level radiation poses little threat.

Obviously, scientists cannot experiment on people to see how low-level radiation affects them. This is where animal experimentation enters the picture. Dr. Fritz and other scientists expose animals to various kinds of radiation, including low-level radiation. If the animals get cancer, the scientists note the kinds of tumors involved and the doses it took to produce them. Many more animal tests and statistical studies are needed before scientists can tell us whether common forms of low-level radiation pose a threat.

Radiation and food are two major research topics among those who are trying to identify cancer causers. Researchers are also studying certain viruses, chemicals, and other substances to see if they should be added to the list of known carcinogens.

The Mechanisms of Cancer

Why does one person get cancer while another with the same lifestyle remains healthy? How does cancer take root in the body? What are the step-by-step events in the disease's development? During the past few years researchers have begun learning about the mechanisms of cancer. Once their understanding is complete, they may be able to save people from cancer by avoiding or interrupting the cancer-producing process.

One recent idea to emerge from animal research is that some cancers may involve a two-step process called *initiation and promotion.* Initiation exposes a person to a carcinogen that somehow makes him or her prone to cancer. Later the person may be exposed to a carcinogen that actually promotes, or brings about, the cancer. In some cases the same substance may serve as both initiator and promoter, with a period of time separating the two episodes.

Since smoking alone can cause cancer, cigarettes are thought to contain both initiators and promoters. Asbestos alone does not seem to cause cancer, but smokers who have had long exposure to asbestos have nearly one hundred times the chance of getting lung cancer as those who just smoke. In this case, cigarettes are thought to be the initiator and asbestos the promoter.

Researchers are doing further studies on the initiation-promotion concept. One day people who have been exposed to cancer initiators may know which specific promoters to avoid, just as those who are prone to pneumonia avoid cool, damp conditions.

To learn more about other research on cancer mechanisms I flew to San Francisco to visit with Dr. Edwin C. Cadman, Director of the Cancer Research Institute at the University of California-San Francisco. Dr. Cadman explained that extremely tiny cellular structures called *oncogenes* are thought to play a role in the development of cancer.

Dr. Edwin C. Cadman

Every cell of the body contains thousands of very tiny genes inherited from one's parents. Our genes determine our eye color, height, and other physical traits. Dr. Cadman said that recent research reveals that oncogenes may be normal genes that have gone haywire.

Embryos have what may be called *developmental genes,* which send the message for them to grow inside their mothers. After early development, these genes are done with their useful work. "However, sometimes these genes are switched on later in life [by certain chemicals, radiation, and other cancer agents] when they're not supposed to be on," Dr. Cadman continued. At this point, the developmental genes are known as *oncogenes.* (*Onco* comes from Greek and means "cancer.") The oncogenes cause uncontrolled cell division—cancer—to develop.

The oncogene concept, which many researchers are now studying, could explain why cancer often runs in families. Just as some families have genes that make their members tall or red-haired, some may have developmental genes that tend to turn into oncogenes. Oncogenes have already been found in many types of tumors.

The Prevention of Cancer

Oncogenes may provide doctors with ways to control or even prevent cancer. "When we learn to turn the oncogenes' switches off, we will be able to keep a cancer from spreading or even from starting," continued Dr. Cadman. "I think we will develop drugs to turn off the switches by 1995."

Dr. Thomas Spelsberg, Professor of Biochemistry at Mayo Medical School in Rochester, Minnesota, agreed that doctors may one day stop or prevent cancer by tampering with oncogenes. There may be several ways to do this, Dr. Spelsberg explained. Certain hormones or drugs could be directed against the oncogenes to switch them off. It may be possible to remove or correct oncogenes —especially if they are proved to have no value once a person is

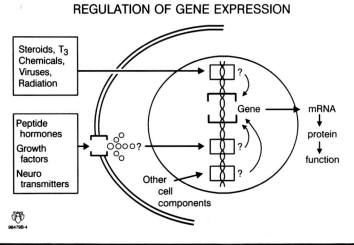

Dr. Thomas Spelsberg (left) and a chart (right) explaining how gene expression is regulated

past the embryo stage. Or perhaps oncogenes could somehow be put into "reverse" to make cancer cells return to normal cells.

Several difficult questions must be answered before doctors can control oncogenes, Dr. Spelsberg continued. Where are the oncogenes located among the thousands of other genes in each cell? How many of these genes are there? How can a normal developmental gene be distinguished from one that will become an oncogene and produce cancer? Is there a complex sequence of events, much like a computer program, that "turns on" the oncogenes? Dr. Spelsberg and dozens of other scientists are looking for the answers to these questions.

Placing oncogenes aside, a number of everyday vitamins and other substances are thought to help prevent cancer. Among these are vitamins A, C, and E, beta-carotene, and the element selenium. Scientists do not know exactly how or why, but studies show that these substances help people avoid the dread disease. For example, a study of eight thousand Norwegians (including smokers and non-smokers) showed that people who consume large amounts of vitamin A have one-sixth the chance of getting lung cancer as those who consume low amounts. In Mexico and Colombia, the lung cancer rate is just one-tenth that in the United States, due perhaps to the extra selenium in those nations' soil and drinking water.

The use of foods, vitamins, and other substances to prevent cancer is a new field called *chemoprevention.* Tests are being made to reveal more about how larger-than-average doses of vitamins A, C, and E, beta-carotene, selenium, and several other substances may help us avoid cancer. It may also interest you to know that spinach, broccoli, and other vegetables that are "good for you" seem to contain some cancer-preventing substances.

Cancer researchers have also noted that people who suffer repeated infections have a much greater than average chance of one day getting cancer. This shows that cancer is somehow related to immunological problems. According to one theory, cancer cells often form in the tissues of *all* people. The immune systems of most of us are able to destroy the young cancer cells. However, in those with defective immune systems, the young cancer cells sometimes escape detection and take root. Researchers are looking for ways to stimulate the immune systems of potential cancer victims so that they can "fight off" the disease like people with normal immune systems.

It may take until well beyond the year 2000 for doctors to learn how to control oncogenes and boost people's immune systems. Still, doctors say that people can take some actions right now to help prevent future cancers:

- *Since about 30 percent of all cancer deaths are related to tobacco use, DON'T SMOKE!*
- *Avoid fatty foods (doing so also helps prevent heart disease)*
- *Avoid X rays unless absolutely necessary*
- *Do not expose yourself to dangerous chemicals or radiation in your home or workplace*
- *Avoid excessive sunlight and wear protective clothing and sunscreen lotions when out in the Sun*

Improved Methods of Diagnosis

During my visit with him at the Mayo Clinic, Dr. Charles Moertel explained that surgery is by far the number one way of "curing" cancer. "Of the 40 percent who are 'cured' of cancer, 99 percent are 'cured' through surgery, not counting the leukemias and lymphomas," said the cancer specialist. Because doctors have the best chance of removing all traces of cancer before it has spread, early detection is the key to successful cancer surgery. A number of tests have been designed to detect cancer in its first stages, but these tests have many problems.

"An early detection test for cancer must meet three requirements to be effective," Dr. Moertel explained. "It must be sensitive enough to find the cancer at an early stage, specific enough not to confuse cancer with other conditions, and inexpensive enough for people to afford." Tests that meet these three standards are lacking for many forms of cancer. As an example, Dr. Moertel mentioned colon cancer, a malignancy for which early detection often means the difference between life and death. When found early, colon cancer is cured nearly 90 percent of the time. However, once the cancer has spread from the colon, the cure rate drops to less than 5 percent.

Dr. Moertel thinks that the popular hemoccult tests, which analyze sample stools (bowel movements) for the hidden blood that sometimes indicates colon cancer, are not very good. "They miss a third to a half of all colon cancers, so they're not very sensitive. Last week a guy came to me who is dying of advanced colon cancer. His doctor had thought he was fine because he'd had a negative hemoccult test. By the time the poor fellow showed up here the cancer had spread to his liver and now he's dying. Not only does the hemoccult test miss quite a few tumors, up to 20 percent of the time the test comes out positive when no tumor is present."

In cooperation with doctors at the University of Minnesota, Dr. Moertel's Mayo Clinic colleagues have devised the hemoquant test, a far more sensitive and specific search for hidden blood than the hemoccult test. Currently the hemoquant test is being tried among high-risk colon cancer candidates in the midwestern United States. "If it works as well as we think it will, the hemoquant could be recommended to the general population," said Dr. Moertel. A good, simple test for detecting early colon cancer is good news for everyone. In the United States, sixty thousand people die yearly of colon cancer—more than die in car accidents. Nearly all colon cancer deaths could be avoided through early detection.

Better diagnostic methods are also being devised for other cancers. For example, urologist Dr. William Gill and his University of Chicago colleagues have recently begun injecting methylene blue dye into bladders that may contain tumors. Normal bladder tissue is covered by a slippery substance called mucus, so the dye does not stick to it. Because tumor cells are not blanketed by mucus, however, the dye turns them blue. This method will not only help doctors spot bladder tumors (forty thousand of which occur yearly in the United States), but it will also help them make sure that all of the tumor is removed during surgery.

Researchers have recently learned that tumors differ from normal tissue in several distinctive ways. Materials flow through cancerous tissues differently than they do through normal tissue. Tumors also give off different magnetic and heat patterns. Several exciting new machines have been designed to measure these differences. Among them are the Positron Emission Tomography scanner and the Magnetic Resonance Imaging scanner.

To learn about Positron Emission Tomography, I flew out to the world-famous Johns Hopkins Hospital in Baltimore, Maryland. There radiology professor Dr. Jonathan Links showed me the hospital's Positron Emission Tomography scanner (called a PET scanner for short). This amazing machine allows doctors to study the functioning of internal organs.

Dr. Links explained that to do PET scanning, the doctor first injects a radioactive drug into the body. The accumulation of the drug in a tumor or otherwise diseased part of the body differs from that

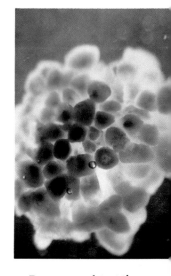

Doctors can detect the presence of tumor cells in a human bladder by observing the cells that absorb blue dye when the bladder is injected with methylene blue dye.

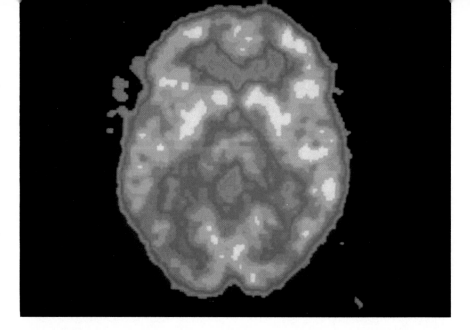

PET image of glucose metabolism in the brain. Yellow and magenta areas indicate the highest level of brain activity.

in healthy tissue. The PET scanner reveals these differences, enabling doctors to spot problems. "PET scanning should be very useful for the early diagnosis and clinical management of many problems, including cancer," explained Dr. Links.

The PET scanning technique is still largely experimental. Dr. Links and other researchers are making a library of PET images to see how various radioactive drugs appear in diseased versus healthy tissue. This will help doctors identify cancerous or otherwise diseased tissue as PET scanning comes into general use.

Magnetic Resonance Imaging (MRI) scanning is another new and growing diagnostic technique. The patient is placed inside the machine, which contains a large magnet. The magnet causes certain magnetic changes in the patient's body. These changes vary depending on whether the tissue being studied is healthy, cancerous, or otherwise diseased. The scanner produces an image that doctors can analyze.

In 1986 there was good news regarding a device called the magnetic resonance (MR) spectrometer, which is similar to the MRI scanner. Researchers at Harvard Medical School and at Boston's Beth Israel Hospital used the MR spectrometer to make chemical tests on blood samples from more than three hundred people. In nearly all cases the MR spectrometer detected tiny differences in the blood of those who were later found to be in the first stages of cancer. This blood test does not reveal the specific kind of cancer that is involved. However, when doctors know that a patient is in the first stages of cancer, they can make further tests to determine where the cancer is. If additional experiments on the MR blood test are successful, it may revolutionize cancer diagnosis by the 1990s.

Improved Methods of Cancer Treatment

There are two reasons why there may never be a "magic bullet" to cure all cancers. Cancer appears in hundreds of forms that strike every part of the body except the hair and the nails. This means that a variety of "cures" may be needed. Even more important, doctors wonder if they will ever be able to wipe out cancer completely in cases where it has spread throughout the body. Although oncogene control or another method *may* allow them to one day conquer all cancers, most doctors say that for the near future it is more realistic to talk about "improved treatment methods" rather than "cure."

Because early detection is crucial, the improved diagnostic methods already described will naturally result in better success against cancer. In addition, researchers are working on a number of promising new treatments.

New chemotherapeutic substances are always being tested for effectiveness against cancer. In fact, people are so eager for anticancer chemicals that a drug can make the headlines just by showing a little promise. Later, people are disappointed to find that the new drug is not the cure-all it was expected to be. For example, in the early 1980s there was great hope that the substance interferon, a protein produced naturally by the healthy body and also synthetically to fight infection, would be a "magic bullet" against all cancers. It has not been a magic bullet, but interferon has helped with several rare forms of leukemia, and in that way has earned a place in the arsenal of cancer-fighting drugs.

Currently doctors are excited about chemotherapeutic agents

produced naturally by the body. The idea is that, since cancer seems to involve a breakdown of the immune system, introducing substances made by a healthy immune system will help fight cancer. Interferon produced by the body, for instance, is an example of such a substance.

In late 1985 Dr. Steven Rosenberg of the National Cancer Institute announced that the natural substance interleukin-2 (a growth factor) showed great promise. Tested on twenty-five advanced cancer patients, interleukin-2 shrank about half the tumors by at least 50 percent and seemed to have "cured" one patient completely. Continuing tests will reveal just how effective interleukin-2 will be.

Monoclonal antibodies are at the heart of another approach using bodily substances. Antibodies are special proteins in the blood that have the ability to seek out and destroy foreign substances. To create monoclonal antibodies, animals are inoculated with certain substances from cancer cells. This stimulates the formation of many antibodies, some of which have the specific ability to seek out cancer cells. The antibody-producing cells are removed from the animals and cultured. The cells are then screened to determine what kind of antibody they are producing. Antibodies that specifically recognize cancer cells are selected out and grown to produce large amounts of cancer-fighting antibodies, which are called *monoclonal antibodies* because they are all identical.

The monoclonal antibodies by themselves have cancer-fighting ability in some cases. Because they seek out cancer cells, the monoclonal antibodies can also be used as messengers to carry cancer-fighting agents directly to tumors. Monoclonal antibodies seem to hold much promise in killing cancer cells of the colon, pancreas, and stomach. More tests are needed, however, before their full value can be determined.

Instead of searching for new therapies, some doctors are trying to discover the best possible combinations for using the known cancer therapies. For example, it could be that drugs, X-ray treatment, and surgery cannot do much against a certain tumor when used sepa-

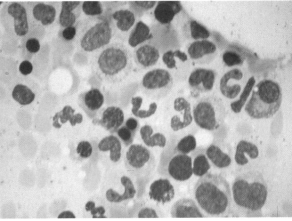

Left: Dr. Gerald Gilchrist. Above: Photo of normal bone marrow after treatment to eliminate leukemia cells

rately. Yet when used together (known as *combination therapy*), they may do a great job.

Dr. Gerald Gilchrist, Chairman of Mayo Clinic's Department of Pediatrics, explained that the great progress doctors have made against leukemia is in large part due to drugs used in combination. He also explained that doctors who treat leukemia patients throughout the United States are now involved in comparing the effectiveness of eight separate combinations of drugs, so that leukemia treatment can be further improved.

Doctors are searching for the best "recipes" for treating many other forms of cancer besides leukemia. Since cancer seems to develop through a complex series of events, the disease may often need to be treated with an equally complex series of cancer-fighting techniques.

Chapter 11
Combating Cardiovascular Disease

I was on the train going to work when all of a sudden there was an intense pressure in my chest, as if an elephant were sitting on it. Also, my left arm felt so weak I couldn't hold my briefcase with it. Having read about it, I knew right away that it was a heart attack. I went to my doctor, and he put me in the hospital. I was there for a full month. After I got out, I felt weak for a long time. Some of my strength came back, but to this day [14 years later] I don't have nearly the energy that I had before my attack.

Heart attack survivor

He [her husband] was a friendly, outgoing guy. He belonged to different organizations, and he liked to exercise at the gym. We had a good social life together, going to dinner and plays and things like that. Then in July of 1981 he had two massive strokes. He lost the use of his right arm completely, and of his right leg somewhat. He can't read or write anymore. He can think a lot better than most people realize, but his talking is very garbled, and it takes a lot of patience to try to understand him. He gets frustrated when he's trying to tell you something and he can't make himself understood. He can only walk if someone helps him. About all he can do is watch TV.

Wife of a stroke victim

Cardiovascular (heart and blood vessel) disease is the number one cause of death among human beings, killing over a million people yearly in the United States alone. Most of these fatalities are among the elderly, but some heart attack and stroke deaths also occur among people in their fifties or younger. Unfortunately, these facts only tell part of the story. Many survivors of heart attacks and strokes spend their last years crippled, bedridden, and depressed.

Although cardiovascular disease kills more people than does

cancer, less research is done on it than is done on cancer. The reason for this is that much less is known about cancer. Nonetheless, hundreds of researchers are working to find better ways of preventing, diagnosing, and treating cardiovascular disease.

Preventing Heart Attacks and Strokes

To learn what is happening in the field of heart attack and stroke prevention, I flew down to the Humana Heart Institute in Louisville, Kentucky. I visited there with Dr. Richard D. Allen, a prominent cardiologist (heart specialist). Dr. Allen said that it has long been known that cigarette smoking, a fatty diet, and lack of exercise are bad for the heart. Because of the recent interest in "staying in shape," more Americans than ever are now protecting their hearts (and entire bodies) by eating well, exercising, and choosing not to smoke.

"Due to better diet, regular exercise, and the decline in smoking we are seeing the amount of heart disease falling off," said Dr. Allen. "If we keep working in that direction, hopefully there will continue to be a gradual decline in heart disease."

Dr. Allen explained that there is another simple way for people to

Good diet and regular exercise can help prevent heart disease.

145

reduce their risk of heart attack and stroke. They can regularly take small doses of aspirin. Studies made in the 1970s and 1980s proved that people who regularly take aspirin suffer fewer heart attacks and strokes than people who don't take aspirin. "Aspirin does this by inhibiting the formation of blood clots," said Dr. Allen. Blood clots lead to heart attacks and strokes by blocking arteries. "Most cardiologists today are putting most of their patients on aspirin. I take one baby aspirin every day and I also advise many of my patients and friends to do so."

About the time that I visited Dr. Allen in summer of 1986, Dr. C. Everett Koop, U.S. Surgeon General, advised people forty and older to take an aspirin each day to prevent cardiovascular disease. Perhaps "aspirin therapy"—which is becoming quite popular—will contribute to the "decline in heart disease" hoped for by Dr. Allen and everyone else.

It must be added that aspirin in large quantities can be deadly and in small amounts can irritate the stomach. Also, about one person in 25,000 is allergic to aspirin and should avoid it. For these reasons, people should talk to their doctors before regularly taking aspirin. Children should NEVER take aspirin or any other drug without being told to by their doctors or parents. Every day, many children are rushed to hospitals because of aspirin overdoses.

Dr. Allen also said that a common food seems to offer protection against heart disease, although the actual value is still uncertain. Researchers have found that people who eat at least two fish meals weekly or take fish oil capsules daily seem to lessen their risk of not only heart disease, but also cancer. Fish oil may also help arthritis! Chemicals in the fish oils seem to interfere with a number of disease processes. In the case of heart disease, the fish oils are thought to prevent fatty deposits from building up in the arteries and to reduce blood clotting. Fish oil may ease mild arthritis by reducing inflammation-producing chemicals called prostaglandins. Researchers in several countries are trying to learn more about how eating fish can help keep us healthy.

Improved Methods of Diagnosis

As with cancer, early diagnosis is crucial in treating cardiovascular disease. If doctors know that a person is susceptible to heart attack or stroke, they may be able to prevent it or at least limit the damage. Doctors have several ways of discovering early cardiovascular problems. They listen to the heart with a stethoscope and make a record of the heartbeat with a device called an electrocardiograph. They can inject dye into the heart (called *cardiac catheterization*) and blood vessels (called *coronary angiogram*) and then observe them for abnormalities with X rays. Several blood tests can also reveal beginning cardiovascular problems. For example, someone whose blood contains too much cholesterol risks heart attack and stroke because this fatty substance blocks blood vessels.

Recently several new ways of detecting cardiovascular problems have been found. It has long been known that a high white blood cell count may mean infection in the body. However, in a six-year study completed in 1982, Dr. Richard H. Grimm Jr. of the University of Minnesota School of Public Health and his colleagues found that people who are likely to have heart attacks also have a rise in their number of white blood cells. Doctors are starting to look at a high white blood cell count as a possible indicator of future heart trouble.

A blood chemistry test can reveal early signs of cardiovascular problems.

147

Two of the most exciting new tools for detecting cardiovascular problems are Positron Emission Tomography (PET) scanning and Magnetic Resonance Imaging (MRI) scanning. MRI produces a better view of some heart structures than can be achieved using other methods. PET scanning yields an outstanding picture of how the heart muscle itself is functioning.

Other methods include echocardiograms that show the structure of the heart and heart valves by using sound waves reflected back from the heart. In addition, there are special monitors that check heartbeat irregularities, nuclear scans that record the strength of the heart's contractions, and treadmill stress tests that measure how the heart works during exercise.

Improved Treatment Methods

New ways of clearing out blocked arteries. Blocked and narrowed arteries are a main cause of heart attacks and strokes. One way to deal with clogged arteries is to perform a coronary artery bypass, which allows the blood to flow around the blockage. A newer method is balloon angioplasty, a technique in which a catheter (thin tube) with a balloon attached to it is inserted into a clogged artery. As the balloon is inflated, the material blocking the artery is pushed against the wall of the artery. To learn about balloon angioplasty

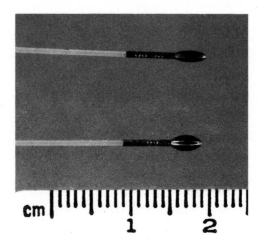

Close-up of a balloon catheter

developments, I met with Dr. Richard Allen, the Humana Heart Institute cardiologist who spoke of aspirin therapy, and also with Dr. John Danforth, a cardiologist at the University of California–San Francisco.

Dr. Allen and Dr. Danforth explained that balloon angioplasty has not replaced the bypass, which is preferable for many patients because of the location of their blockages and their personal anatomy. However, for those who can benefit from balloon angioplasty, it is a much easier procedure than a bypass. "A bypass is a major operation," said Dr. Danforth. "Following a successful balloon angioplasty, the patient is often out of the hospital the next day."

"Balloon angioplasty has a high success rate for clearing out blockages—greater than 90 percent," Dr. Allen added. "Since about 1985, we have even been doing balloon angioplasty on people who are actually *having* a heart attack. If we can get them to us within two to four hours we can open up the arteries and in a lot of instances stop the heart attack and save the heart muscle."

Both doctors said that new and better materials are always being developed for balloon angioplasty. This enables cardiologists to do angioplasty on more complex cases. "New balloons that can withstand more pressure are always being developed, and they allow us to use higher pressures on difficult blockages," said Dr. Allen. "The guide wires [which guide the balloon through the catheter] are also constantly being improved. The improved guide wires can make turns and go at sharp angles that the old ones couldn't, allowing us to do cases we couldn't attempt before. Just this morning I cleared a completely blocked artery that I couldn't have done just a few years ago."

Dr. Allen and Dr. Danforth both mentioned another way of clearing out blocked arteries. It involves using a laser (a device that sends a thin but powerful beam of light) to burn away blockages in arteries. So far, laser angioplasty, as it is called, has been used on small numbers of human beings, usually successfully. "I think that in a few years lasers will be used in combination with balloon open clogged arteries," predicted Dr. Danforth, "and we hope that by the year 2000 lasers by themselves will be able to burn through the blockages altogether."

The mechanical heart. One way to help people with failing hearts is to give them good ones taken from dead people. Heart transplantation, which will be discussed later, has a big drawback. "There aren't enough hearts to go around," explained Dr. Allan M. Lansing, Director of the Humana Heart Institute in Louisville, Kentucky.

"About five hundred heart transplants are done per year in the United States," continued Dr. Lansing. "Even if we doubled or tripled the number of available hearts it wouldn't solve the shortage problem, because at least 30,000 people each year could benefit from a new heart in the United States.

"One way to deal with this problem is to use animal hearts. That is being researched now, but it is still many years off. The other way to replace a damaged heart is to use a mechanical device—the mechanical heart."

As long ago as the 1930s several scientists tried to construct mechanical hearts. One of the most promising artificial hearts was developed at the University of Utah in Salt Lake City between the late

The Jarvik-7 mechanical heart

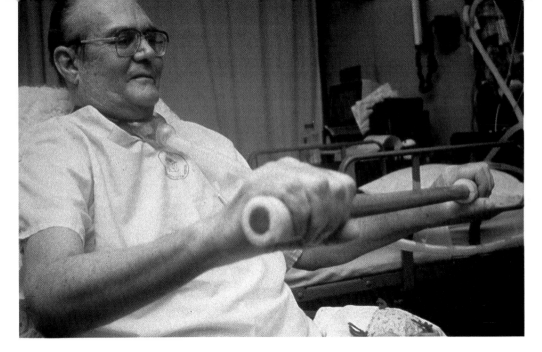

1960s and the early 1980s. It was named the *Jarvik-7* after its designer, Dr. Robert Jarvik.

The Jarvik-7 is made of plastic and metal and weighs half a pound. Leading out of the heart are two plastic hoses, which exit through two openings made in the patient's abdomen and attach to a machine called the *heart driver.* By forcing air through the plastic hoses and into the artificial heart at regular intervals, the heart driver causes the Jarvik-7 to pump blood. Experiments with animals showed that the Jarvik-7 worked well. By 1982 University of Utah doctors led by Dr. William C. DeVries were ready to implant the Jarvik-7 in a human being.

Doctors avoid trying risky new treatments on patients who can be helped by older, proved methods. For that reason, University of Utah doctors did not want to implant the Jarvik-7 in anyone who could be helped by a heart transplant, drugs, or any other standard treatment. Instead they looked for an "end-stage" heart patient—someone who would die unless an unusual treatment were tried.

Dr. Barney Clark, a Seattle dentist, was selected to receive the first artificial heart. On December 2, 1982, a surgical team headed by Dr. DeVries opened Clark's chest, removed his heart, connected the Jarvik-7 to his circulatory system, and sewed it into place.

Considering that Clark had been near death before the operation, his artificial heart implantation was quite successful. Despite complications, within several weeks he could sit up, watch TV, read, and even walk a short way—always attached, of course, to his heart driver. However, 112 days after receiving his Jarvik-7, several of Barney Clark's organs failed and he died. The artificial heart was still working properly at his death.

Since then, several other end-stage heart patients have received Jarvik-7's. To learn about them and about the future of the mechanical heart, I spent a day at the world's leading artificial heart center—the Humana Heart Institute in Louisville, Kentucky. The Institute's Director, Dr. Allan M. Lansing, who earlier gained fame for performing the world's first human spleen transplant, discussed the artificial heart with me.

"The Humana Heart Institute is paying for the first one hundred artificial heart implantations done here," said Dr. Lansing. "After one hundred, we will know whether or not the artificial heart is of value."

In 1984 Dr. William DeVries joined the Humana Heart Institute staff, and by April of 1985 he had implanted Jarvik-7's in three patients there. Although none resumed a normal life, all three lived longer than they would have without the Jarvik-7. One patient lived

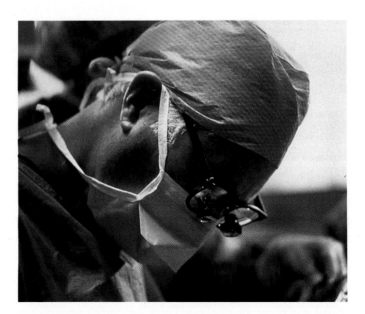

Dr. Allan Lansing

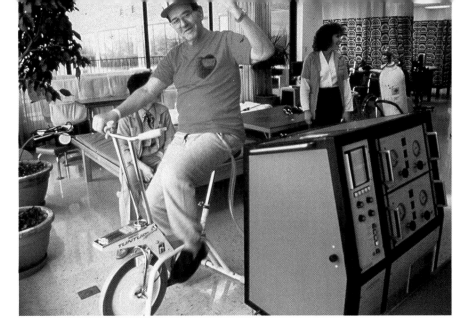

ten days, another a year and four months, and the third a year and eight months. All three suffered from complications, some having nothing to do with the Jarvik-7.

"The Jarvik-7's reliability and durability have been proven," continued Dr. Lansing. "There have been no failures of the pumping mechanism or the valves—in other words, no mechanical failures. The Jarvik-7 does have some problems, however. We want to improve the materials it's made of, so that the body will accept it more readily. We want to improve the valves and the inner lining so that blood clots will be less likely, and we want to miniaturize the heart itself. All of these are relatively easy. The biggest challenge is to come up with an implantable power supply."

By "implantable power supply," Dr. Lansing means a power source that can be placed inside the patient's chest. This would allow the patient to move around more easily and would also help solve the problem of infection.

"The tubes [leading from the patient's body to the heart driver] promote infection," Dr. Lansing explained. "Bacteria grow from the patient's skin surface down the tubes and toward the heart. Eventually all of the patients have experienced some infection." An implantable power supply in the chest would remove the need for the infection-causing tubes. Dr. Lansing said that several private science research firms are working on an implantable power supply—in the form of batteries that could be recharged from outside the chest by special coils.

The Jarvik-7 and other mechanical hearts now being developed are very controversial. Some scientists say that mechanical hearts will never improve the quality or length of life enough to be worthwhile. These scientists say that the time and money spent on mechanical hearts would be better spent on other kinds of research.

Others, the believers in the mechanical heart, say that work on these devices is still in its infancy and that total success cannot be expected so soon. Boosters of the artificial heart predict that fifty or one hundred years from now end-stage heart patients will routinely be returned to near-normal lives by these devices, much as an old car can be made to run better by replacing a faulty part. Another plus for mechanical hearts is that they can serve as "bridges" to keep heart patients alive while they await heart transplants. This has already been done—for the most part successfully—on several dozen patients.

New drugs. Drugs will always be important tools for treating cardiovascular ailments, despite advances that may be made in heart transplantation, mechanical hearts, and other kinds of surgery. The reasons for this are that some ailments are best treated without surgery and that some people are poor prospects for surgery.

Dozens of cardiovascular medications are now in common use. These include drugs to strengthen the heartbeat, steady the heartbeat, reduce blood pressure, open the blood vessels, and lower blood levels of cholesterol. There are also substances that can be injected into the veins to dissolve a fresh clot in the coronary blood vessel of someone having a heart attack. Researchers are always testing possible new heart medications, and from time to time they find one that works. Before a new drug can come into general use in the United States, it must undergo rigorous tests, including animal trials and tests on human patients who cannot be helped by standard methods.

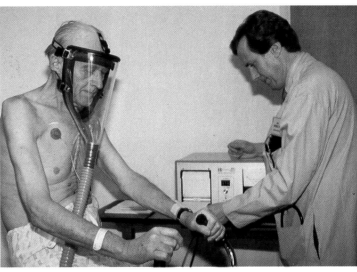

Left: Dr. Chatterjee.
Right: Dr. Weber

To learn about promising new drugs I spoke to Dr. Kanu Chatterjee, a University of California–San Francisco cardiologist, and also to Dr. Karl Weber, Director of Michael Reese Hospital's Cardiovascular Institute in Chicago. Both men said that some outstanding heart medications have recently been developed.

Enoximone and Milrinone are the names of two promising new drugs for victims of acute heart failure. In tests on patients who did not respond to other drugs, Enoximone and Milrinone improved the pumping function of the heart and also helped open up the blood vessels so that blood could flow through them easier. What this means in human terms is that some heart patients who once got exhausted walking to the mailbox can now live near-normal lives thanks to these drugs.

"Both Enoximone and Milrinone have improved the quality of people's lives, but they are both still in the experimental stage in selected medical centers," explained Dr. Weber. If tests with Enoximone and Milrinone continue to prove positive, they should come into general use. These and other drugs now being developed should help millions of heart patients live better lives without having to undergo surgery.

Chapter 12
The Conquest of Disease

When we feel our strength failing our only consolation is to tell ourselves that we can help our successors to do more than we have done, and do it better, by marching with their eyes on the distant horizons which we were able only to glimpse.

Louis Pasteur

Cancer and heart disease receive the most attention from researchers because they kill the most people. Nevertheless, progress is also being made against many of the thousands of other human diseases. The following are some major diseases for which a great deal of research is now being done.

Malaria

Malaria, a disease that causes chills and high fever, has always been a dreaded killer of human beings. In past centuries, hundreds of thousands of people died of malaria each year in India alone. Malaria epidemics also claimed tens of thousands of lives yearly in many other nations in Africa, Asia, Central and South America, and parts of Europe.

One reason for malaria's deadliness was that people did not know how it was spread. It was widely thought that malaria came from breathing stale air. (The word *malaria* is Italian meaning "bad air.") Only at the end of the nineteenth century did scientists learn that malaria is caused by tiny, one-celled animals called *Plasmodia* protozoans that are spread from person to person by *Anopheles* mosquitoes.

Understanding its causes enabled people to combat malaria. Throughout the twentieth century many stagnant bodies of water that were breeding areas for *Anopheles* mosquitoes have been drained; powerful insecticides such as DDT have been directed

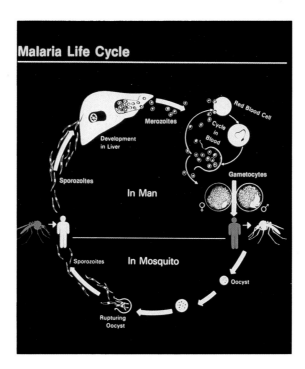

Malaria Life Cycle

Red Blood Cell

Merozoites

Cycle in Blood

Development in Liver

Sporozoites

Gametocytes

In Man

♀ ♂

In Mosquito

Sporozoites

Oocyst

Rupturing Oocyst

Drawing shows the life cycle of the Anopheles *mosquito*

against the mosquitoes; and screens have been put up in malarial areas to keep the mosquitoes out. These measures have helped control malaria, but they have not wiped out the disease.

One problem is that it is almost impossible to kill all the *Anopheles* mosquitoes. Also, the malaria-spreading mosquitoes have become resistant to the insecticides aimed at them, and some forms of *Plasmodia* have become resistant to the drugs used in treating the disease. As a result, each year about 300 million of the world's people get malaria, mainly in Africa, Asia, and Central and South America; about 1½ million of them die of malaria and its complications.

To learn what is being done to combat malaria I phoned the Malaria Branch of the United States Centers for Disease Control (CDC) in Atlanta, Georgia. Dr. Alan Greenberg, a CDC epidemiologist (specialist on the occurrence of disease among large numbers of people), explained that swamp draining and the use of insecticides to kill the mosquitoes are still standard ways of preventing malaria. However, perhaps the most exciting news is that researchers are working on vaccines to prevent malaria.

A person would be injected with an antigen (a substance that can stimulate the immune system) associated with malaria. The antigen would cause the person to produce antibodies against malaria. If exposed to malaria later, the person would have a supply of antibodies ready to fight off the disease. Dr. Greenberg said that researchers in the United States, Europe, and Australia are working on vaccines to stop malaria at three key stages of the disease's complex cycle:

Vaccine #1: Malaria is transmitted when a female *Anopheles* mosquito injects *Plasmodia* protozoans into a person. The *Plasmodia* are what make the victim sick. A vaccine aimed at this stage would prevent malaria by killing the *Plasmodia* as soon as the mosquito injected them into the victim.

Vaccine #2: The *Plasmodia* make the victim sick by invading red blood cells and then multiplying inside them. This destroys the red blood cells. A vaccine aimed at this stage would prevent malaria by interfering with *Plasmodia* multiplication.

Vaccine #3: This vaccine would not protect the victim from getting malaria, but it would help stop the spread of the disease. In the victim's bloodstream, some of the *Plasmodia* develop into male and female cells. If the victim is bitten by another *Anopheles* mosquito, the male and female *Plasmodia* reproduce inside the mosquito's stomach. These new *Plasmodia* can be injected into another person during the mosquito's next blood meal. A vaccine targeted against this stage would stimulate the immune system to attack the *Plasmodia* before they could divide into the male and female cells.

Dr. Marguerite Pappaioanou, another CDC Malaria Branch epidemiologist, explained that the trick is to find a part of *Plasmodia* that can inspire antibody production in the bloodstream without harming the person. Since *Plasmodia* contain hundreds of separate parts, or antigens, that task is not easy. Also, an antigen that would make a good vaccine must be separated from the rest of the *Plasmodia* and duplicated in large quantities.

Dr. Ruth Nussenzweig and her husband Dr. Victor Nussenzweig, both of New York University Medical Center, head a research team

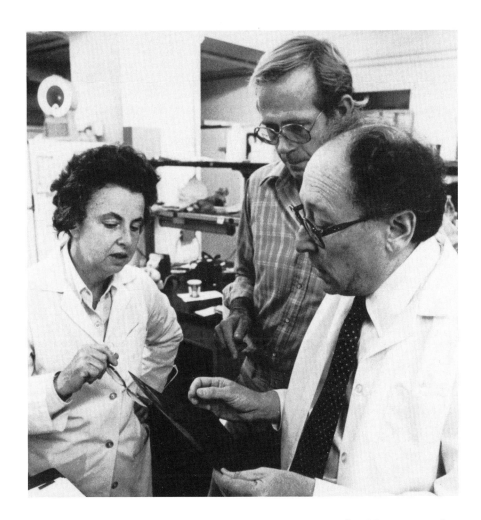

Doctors Victor and Ruth Nussenzweig

that is making progress on a malaria vaccine. The Nussenzweigs have learned the chemical makeup of the main antigen involved in stage one of malaria. They are now producing large amounts of this antigen. When injected into people, this antigen would stimulate production of antibodies that would protect them from malaria.

Hopefully the researchers working on vaccines for all three stages will succeed. If they do, all three vaccines may be combined into one powerhouse malaria vaccine. That would be great news for the approximately 300 million people who catch malaria annually, and could save the lives of the 1½ million who now die of malaria and its complications each year.

Influenza

Many people think of influenza (often called "the flu") as a mild disease involving a few days of fever, chills, headaches, and body aches. In most cases, influenza *is* just that. However, influenza can also weaken people to the point that pneumonia and other diseases may set in and cause serious illness or even death. From 1918 to 1919 a worldwide influenza epidemic killed more than 25 million people, including half a million in the United States. This was one of the five deadliest epidemics of any kind in history. There have been many other flu epidemics in which hundreds of thousands of people have died, and even today influenza kills hundreds of thousands of people around the world each year.

Doctors have two main ways of controlling influenza. Antibiotics and other drugs protect people from pneumonia and other diseases that can strike after a bout with the flu. Doctors have also developed influenza vaccines, but the problem with these is that the flu comes in many forms. A vaccine made from one influenza virus will not provide much protection against other forms of the virus. Since new forms of the virus are always developing, a new type of vaccine must be made every year.

I spoke to Nancy Arden, an epidemiologist at the CDC's Influenza Branch, in hopes of learning that progress is being made against this disease. Ms. Arden explained that until recently only dead viruses were used in creating influenza vaccines. Doctors have now begun using live (but weakened) influenza viruses in vaccines. Live viruses appear to have several big advantages over dead ones when used in influenza vaccines. "They may provide longer-lasting immunity and offer better protection, but that is still under study," said Ms. Arden. "Also, the live ones can be administered more easily than the dead ones. The killed viruses have to be given by injection, which takes a trained person to administer. The live ones are sprayed or dropped into the nose, which is much easier to administer, and which most people prefer to getting a shot."

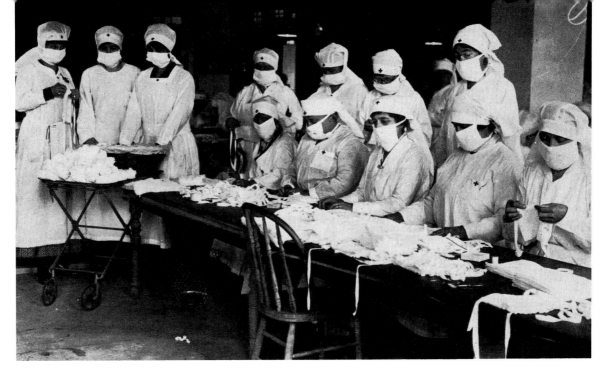

Red Cross workers make gauze masks during the great influenza epidemic of 1918

Health officials in several countries, including Russia, Yugoslavia, and Czechoslovakia, are so convinced of the superiority of live flu vaccines that they are already using them. In the United States, however, which has one of the world's most cautious systems for testing new medicines, live vaccines have not yet been approved by the Food and Drug Administration (FDA). Currently the live vaccines are being tested on people in the United States. If these tests prove that live viruses work better than dead ones, health officials in the United States will begin using the live flu vaccines.

In the world's poor countries, live influenza vaccines could save tens of thousands of lives each year—if one problem can be overcome. The vaccine must be kept cool. Some countries do not have the refrigeration systems to preserve the vaccine while it is being distributed to distant villages.

The live flu vaccines share one major problem with the dead ones, Nancy Arden explained. "That sneaky trick the flu virus has of changing would mean that one vaccine couldn't protect you from all forms of the disease." As a result, influenza will probably always be with us to a certain degree, meaning that better ways for treating the disease are needed.

Since the 1960s, the drug amantadine has been used to treat some kinds of influenza. Amantadine is effective in preventing illness if given before someone has the flu and can help a person who is already sick recover faster. However, some people who take amantadine suffer upset stomach and other side effects.

During the last few years rimantadine (a drug related to amantadine) has come into use in Russia and several other countries. "Rimantadine does the same things as amantadine with fewer people having side effects," said Nancy Arden. In the United States, rimantadine has passed animal tests and is now being tested on people. It will probably be licensed in the United States before 1990. Together, the improved vaccines and drugs should help reduce the death toll from influenza in years to come.

Diabetes

Insulin is the main hormone that regulates the body's use of sugar. Some people's bodies either do not produce enough insulin or cannot properly use insulin. These people suffer from diabetes. If untreated, diabetics accumulate too much sugar in their blood. Victims of the more serious form of the disease—juvenile diabetes—are especially vulnerable and can die without daily insulin injections. Even with treatment, diabetics are prone to develop a number of health problems. Millions of the world's people die of diabetes each year, including more than 100,000 in the United States.

One new treatment that has come into widespread use for diabetics is "genetically engineered" insulin, which is made with the help of bacteria in an interesting process discussed in Chapter 14. To learn about other progress being made against diabetes, I spoke to Dr. Deborah Edidin, an endocrinologist (expert on the pancreas and other endocrine glands) at Evanston Hospital in Evanston, Illinois.

Regarding a cure, Dr. Edidin said that researchers are working to perfect the pancreas transplant (over two hundred of which have been done). Since the pancreas produces insulin, replacing the diabetic's faulty pancreas with a healthy one should theoretically

Dr. Deborah Edidin

cure the disease. "However, not enough pancreases are available for all who need them and rejection of the new pancreas is also a problem," explained Dr. Edidin. "There is another problem. We don't know whether a virus, stress, or other factors cause diabetes, but we do know that some people have genes which make them disposed towards diabetes. This means that even if we could obtain enough pancreases and avoid rejection we would still have to deal with the genetic factors that caused the person to get diabetes in the first place. Those genetic factors may cause the person to get diabetes again despite the new pancreas." Dr. Edidin added that diabetes has recurred in some patients who have received pancreas transplants.

Turning to another possible cure, Dr. Edidin explained that non-diabetic people produce insulin in the area of the pancreas called the *islets of Langerhans*. In animal experiments, islets from a healthy pancreas have continued to produce insulin when injected into a second animal. Several researchers are now injecting islet cells from living and dead humans into diabetic persons to see if this will help them produce insulin. A few problems need to be solved, however, before islet injection can come into widespread use for diabetics.

"There is a problem with rejection, the same as with a pancreas transplant," explained Dr. Edidin. "There is a problem with determining the amount of islets needed, and there is a problem with obtaining the islets." She added that besides islets from humans, islets from animal donors may be usable. It is hoped that these problems will soon be solved so that islet transplantation can be used to control diabetes.

The method that many people feel will be best for treating diabetes, however, is the artificial pancreas, continued Dr. Edidin. "We already have an exterior pump that can deliver insulin, but it cannot determine the level of the person's blood sugar, so it doesn't know how much insulin to deliver. Researchers are working on a miniature, artificial pancreas that could be implanted inside the patient. A sensor would tell the amount of sugar in the patient's blood and the pump would release the proper amount of insulin into the body based on that reading." Dr. Edidin concluded by saying that Japanese and American scientists are making progress on building an artificial pancreas.

Arthritis

Arthritis is a general term describing more than one hundred diseases involving stiffness and swelling of the joints. Among the most common of these are osteoarthritis, rheumatoid arthritis, and gout. Although people usually do not die of arthritis, all of its forms are painful and some are potentially crippling. Arthritis is common. Over forty million Americans suffer from one form or another of arthritis, making it the country's most common chronic disease.

I learned about current research on arthritis from two experts—Dr. Robert Katz of Rush-Presbyterian-St. Luke's Medical Center in Chicago and Dr. Daniel Albert of the University of Chicago. Both said that rheumatoid arthritis, called the "great crippler," is a main focus of attention among arthritis researchers.

Traditionally various aspirin-like drugs have been used to relieve the pain and swelling of rheumatoid arthritis. Injections of gold in a thick liquid form may also be used to relieve the symptoms. When

Dr. Robert Katz

joints are very badly damaged by the disease, they can be removed surgically and replaced with artificial joints.

Recently, doctors have learned that a number of drugs used against other diseases also help combat rheumatoid and related forms of arthritis. These include drugs usually targeted against malaria, ulcerative colitis (a disease of the colon), and cancer, with the cancer drugs proving especially effective. Many of these drugs are still experimental in connection with rheumatoid arthritis and are being tested on animals and/or selected human volunteers. "We're finding that some of these drugs are especially effective when used in combination, much as is the case with cancer," explained Dr. Katz. "We're trying to work out the best possible formulas." When doctors learn which of the new drugs work best and in what combinations, thousands of rheumatoid arthritis victims will benefit.

Although drugs can relieve rheumatoid arthritis's symptoms, no known drug can prevent the disease or cure it once it appears. Most experts think that these ultimate goals—preventing and curing

Dr. Daniel Albert

rheumatoid arthritis—will not be achieved until the disease's causes are pinpointed.

Dr. Daniel Albert explained that research on animals and on human patients has provided several clues about those causes. Researchers now think that autoimmunity is involved in rheumatoid arthritis. An autoimmune response is one in which a person produces antibodies that attack his or her own body. In other words, the patient's own body could be giving the order for rheumatoid arthritis to develop. However, an outside force such as a virus or chemical may trigger this reaction, and heredity may determine who has this unusual autoimmune response.

Cancer and AIDS, both of which have attracted far more research than has rheumatoid arthritis, are also thought to involve problems with the immune system. Research on those two diseases is slowly revealing information about the causes of rheumatoid arthritis. Knowing the mechanisms of rheumatoid arthritis may enable doctors to one day conquer the disease.

AIDS

Many people think of the war against disease as a struggle against an unchanging enemy. Germs do change over the years. A drug that kills certain bacteria one year may be less effective ten years later because of resistance developed by the germs. Occasionally, germs that were never seen before, appear, baffling the medical community. Such was the case when an apparently new disease began killing thousands of people in the early 1980s.

In 1980 and 1981 a few young American men developed a mysterious disease. Actually, each suffered from a set of diseases including rare cancers, strange fevers, and other puzzling health problems. It was obvious that their immune systems had been somehow weakened, leaving them prone to an array of illnesses.

In 1981 doctors named this strange disease Acquired Immune Deficiency Syndrome (AIDS). It was *Acquired* because its victims were not born with the disease, but somehow "caught" it. *Immune Deficiency* referred to an immune system problem and *Syndrome* to the fact that AIDS brings on a group of diseases. Never having seen AIDS before, doctors had no weapons against it. AIDS victims always died from all their complications within several years.

Everyone hoped that AIDS would be limited to the few young men who first got it, but soon the disease was claiming dozens, then hundreds, of lives. As AIDS deaths made headlines, a degree of panic spread through the general public. Most people thought that big outbreaks of serious communicable diseases were over—at least in the wealthier countries. What if AIDS started killing hundreds of thousands or even millions of people like the plagues of old? What if the disease occurred as regularly as the common cold?

It was soon learned that AIDS for the most part targeted certain groups. Male homosexuals (men who have sexual relations with other men) were its main victims. Also at risk were people who injected drugs into their veins and those who received blood transfusions. However, doctors did not yet know how or why these people were targeted. Then in 1983 researchers in France found that a virus

U.S. Surgeon General C. Everett Koop (second from left) stands in front of the Coming Home Hospice in San Francisco, a care center for terminally ill AIDS patients.

causes AIDS. The virus, called HIV (human immunodeficiency virus), attacks certain white blood cells that help protect the body against infections and cancers. Scientists then determined why homosexuals, intravenous drug users, and recipients of blood transfusions were prone to contract the disease.

If one of the homosexual partners has AIDS, he can pass the AIDS virus through sexual activity to his partner's bloodstream. Drug users often share one needle when injecting themselves with drugs. If one of the needle sharers has AIDS, he or she can spread the virus through the infected needle to others. Finally, some men, women, and children were infected with AIDS when receiving blood donated by people who had the AIDS virus.

Learning its cause and the ways it was spread were the first steps toward controlling AIDS. Blood from donors is now tested for the AIDS virus. Infected blood is discarded, and only blood that is free of the virus is given to those needing transfusions. Efforts have also been made to inform male homosexuals about the dangers of some sexual practices. In addition, drug users have been warned that they are risking their lives in two ways—from the drugs and also from needles that may be contaminated by AIDS. Nevertheless, despite the efforts of hundreds of scientists, by 1989 no way to cure or prevent AIDS had been found, and the disease was still killing thousands of people each year.

Dozens of drugs are now being tested for use against AIDS, with attention being given to various drug combinations. As for preventing the disease, doctors hope to have a vaccine against AIDS by the early 1990s. One plan being tested involves the cowpox vaccine that wiped out smallpox. The cowpox vaccine would be used to carry bits of genetic material from the AIDS virus into a person's bloodstream. These virus bits would not be strong enough to cause AIDS, but they would stimulate production of antibodies against AIDS. This method will require several years of testing on animals and human volunteers to determine if it works.

The conquest of AIDS has become one of the major goals of medicine. In the United States, where most of the AIDS cases have occurred, nearly 50,000 people had died of the disease by early 1989. Although it appears that AIDS may never become extremely common, there is evidence that it may cease to be mainly a disease of male homosexuals and will be found throughout the general population. The U.S. Department of Health and Human Services estimates that by the end of 1992, 365,000 Americans will have contracted AIDS and that three-fourths of them will be dead by then. If scientists can find ways to prevent and cure AIDS, perhaps these figures will be proved wrong.

Mental Illness

Many people who would see a doctor for pneumonia or a broken arm feel that it is somehow shameful to seek help for mental problems. Because of this, it is difficult to calculate the number of mentally ill people. However, the statistics that are available on mental illness are disturbing. As of 1986 about 12 million Americans, or 5 percent of the nation's people, were thought to be suffering from major depression. In all, nearly one-fifth of all Americans were thought to be suffering from various mental problems that at least somewhat upset their lives.

Another yardstick for measuring mental health is a nation's suicide rate. People must be suffering badly from mental problems to kill themselves, so a high suicide rate means that a large segment of the population is unhappy. In the United States the suicide rate is

Dr. Kathryn Zerbe

rather high—one suicide every twenty minutes, or about thirty thousand per year. Most alarming is the fact that more young Americans than ever are killing themselves. In 1958 people under age thirty-five accounted for 19 percent of all suicides. By the 1980s more than 40 percent of all suicides were committed by people under age thirty-five, and suicide was the third leading cause of death for that age group. A large number of troubled young people is a bad sign for the nation's future mental health.

I spoke to Dr. Kathryn Zerbe, a psychiatrist at the Menninger Clinic in Topeka, Kansas, to learn about new ways of helping the mentally ill. Founded in 1925, the Menninger Clinic has long been considered one of the world's leading psychiatric centers.

Dr. Zerbe explained that each mental illness has its own proper treatment, which means that a patient must be properly diagnosed before he or she can be helped. New medical tests are being developed to help psychiatrists make more accurate diagnoses. Currently attention is being paid to changes in certain hormones and in brain chemicals called *neurotransmitters* in mentally ill people. Doctors are trying to develop simple tests to measure and interpret these changes. If they succeed, these tests would greatly help in psychiatric diagnosis.

It is also crucial to make sure that there is no physical cause for the mental problem, Dr. Zerbe explained. "It has recently been learned that the first complaint of 40 percent of all cancer patients is depression," she said. Many of these people are sent to psychiatrists. Meanwhile their cancer spreads and by the time it's discovered it is too late. Dr. Zerbe added that arthritis sometimes starts with a bout of depression, too, and that sudden anxiety problems may mean the early stages of heart disease. Psychiatrists and other doctors are becoming more aware of these connections, which should lead to better diagnoses of both mental and physical problems.

Dr. Zerbe then discussed some exciting new treatment methods. "New and better drugs are being developed all the time," the psychiatrist said and then listed new drugs for treating depression, manic-depressive illness, anxiety disorders, panic attacks, schizophrenia, phobias, and drug addiction. Generally, these new drugs relieve the symptoms better than the older drugs did, and they also have fewer side effects.

"Besides new drugs, we are experimenting with interesting new ways of helping people with mental problems. Some psychiatrists are doing research on keeping depressed patients up all night, because it seems that depressed people who are deprived of sleep feel better. We call that *sleep deprivation therapy.*" It has also recently been learned that a lack of sunlight causes a hormonal change that can promote depression. "Why this hormonal change affects some people more than others is not known, but those who suffer due to a lack of sunlight get better when they are exposed to more sunlight," Dr. Zerbe explained. A few psychiatrists are even treating their sunlight-deprived patients with special lights that resemble the Sun, and this seems to help, too!

During the twentieth century doctors have learned that mental illnesses, like physical ones, are caused by our environment and heredity. As people realize that mental illnesses have specific causes and are nothing shameful, hopefully more of us will seek help when these problems arise.

Chapter 13

Transplants, Artificial Organs, and *In Vitro* Fertilization

To be able to see the heartbeat of the brain-dead [donor] in-
fant stopped, the heart captured and taken to [the baby who
needs it], and then to see it quivering as if to say, "I have to
beat, let me go, watch me go," and to see it start beating again
and give life to another baby, well, believe me, it's one of the
greatest highs you're ever going to have.

Dr. David Hinshaw, describing a heart
transplant by Dr. Leonard Lee Bailey

Transplants

Transplants using human organs. One wintry night in late 1985 a
young man in Wisconsin committed suicide. Soon after the young
man's death, Dr. Sylvester Sterioff, head of Transplantation Surgery at the Mayo Clinic in Minnesota, was informed about it. Dr.
Sterioff and two assistants boarded a chartered plane and in a short
while they were "harvesting" the young man's organs.

Dr. Sterioff and his team removed the dead body's liver, kidneys,
and eyes. The heart is often harvested, too, but in this case it had
been damaged and could not be used. After immersing the organs
in a special salt solution, the transplant team placed them in plastic
bowls and then placed the bowls inside ordinary picnic coolers. The
organs were taken to the Mayo Clinic and other hospitals, where
they were transplanted into people who needed a new liver and kidneys to live and new eyes to see.

Harvesting organs from dead bodies may seem gruesome, but it
can mean life to people who need new organs. A few years ago the
young man's body would have been buried or cremated without
any consideration given to its possible usefulness. Today before it is
buried or cremated, a dead body in good condition can save the lives

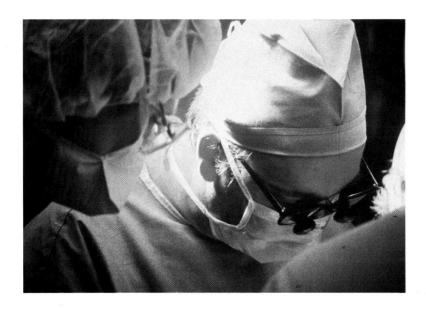

Dr. Sylvester Sterioff

of several people. As Dr. A. Michael Borkon, a transplant surgeon at Johns Hopkins University in Baltimore, Maryland, told me: "We can get corneas [the transparent coverings of the eyes], a heart, two lungs, two kidneys, a liver, a pancreas, bones, and skin from one donor, and they are dispersed to maybe eight or ten people who benefit from the tragedy."

Although the first successful eye cornea transplant was done back in 1905, only in recent years have whole major organs been successfully transplanted. The drug cyclosporine, which came into use in the early 1980s, has been a boon to transplant surgery by helping patients' bodies stop rejecting their new organs. With each passing year, the annual number of transplants increases, as does the success rate.

To learn what is happening with organ transplantation, I met with the Mayo Clinic's Dr. Sterioff and also flew out west to meet with Dr. Oscar Salvatierra, Jr., Chief of the Transplant Service at the University of California–San Francisco.

Both men explained that, although transplantation techniques are always improving, a big ongoing problem is a lack of donor organs. Vital organs, such as the kidneys, heart, and liver, cannot be

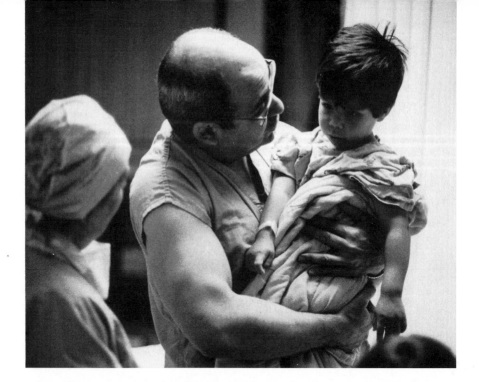

taken from just any dead body, because the organs die soon after the heart has stopped pumping. Instead, most vital organs used in transplants are taken from a donor whose brain is legally dead but whose heart and circulation are artificially maintained. A person who has suffered brain death in this way cannot return to life because his or her brain can no longer work. Each year in the United States, there are more than twenty-five thousand brain death victims who could donate good major organs. Many of them are young adults who have died in traffic accidents or have committed suicide. Only about one-tenth of those organs are actually harvested, however. As a result, each year thousands of sick people die while the organs that could have saved them are not used.

Doctors Sterioff and Salvatierra emphasized that transplant surgeons do not want people to die just so that they can take their organs. "We want people to live," said Dr. Sterioff. "We are trying to prevent accidents, to get people to buckle up, and to save accident victims." However, they also feel that organ donation is one way for something positive to come out of a tragic death. "The thing to remember is that by donating your organs you can give somebody else a second chance at life," Dr. Salvatierra said.

UNIFORM DONOR CARD

Of_____
Print or type name of donor

In the hope that I may help others, I hereby make this anatomical gift, if medically acceptable, to take effect upon my death. The words and marks below indicate my desires.

I give: (a)____any needed organs or parts

       (b)____only the following organs or parts

_____
Specify the organ(s) or part(s)
or
for the purposes of transplantation, therapy, medical research or education:

      (c)____my body for anatomical study if needed.

Limitations, or
special wishes, if any:_____

An organ donor card

People can identify themselves as organ donors in several ways. They can fill out "donor cards" stating that they want to offer their organs in case they die. (The signatures of people under eighteen must be witnessed by a parent or guardian.) In some states organ donors can identify themselves on their drivers' licenses. Also, the family can allow the organs of a dead person to be harvested—unless the deceased had opposed this idea. The problem is that too few people fill out donor cards, and too few families donate the organs of their dead relatives.

Thousands of people would probably fill out the cards if there were simple ways to inform them about organ donation. Methods are now being developed to tell more people about it. Hospitals are now informing families of people who are brain-dead that organ donation is an option. Perhaps in the future people will be routinely offered donor cards when they enter the hospital; laws may even be passed *requiring* hospitals to ask incoming patients about organ donation.

Several technical problems involving organ transplantation are also receiving attention. Most organs are usable (surgeons call it "viable") for just a short while. For example, the heart can be used for about four hours and the liver for about eight hours after being removed from the brain-dead person. Because of this, it is crucial to take the organs where they are needed very quickly. Because no central bureau coordinated the supply of available organs up until the 1980s, many transplant centers wasted precious time trying to track down much-needed organs. Patients sometimes died even though, unknown to the transplant center, organs were available only a short distance away.

To help solve this problem in 1984 the United Network for Organ Sharing (UNOS) was formed by about two hundred hospitals and transplant centers. At the UNOS communications center in Richmond, Virginia, teams of coordinators work around the clock to locate needed organs throughout the United States. Dr. Salvatierra, the organization's president at the time I spoke to him, explained that more patients than ever before are getting the organs they need thanks to UNOS.

Researchers are also making progress in preserving organs for longer time periods. This allows the organs to survive delays until they are used and enables doctors to spend more time operating. Several researchers are even trying to find ways to freeze the heart, liver, and other vital organs without damaging them. Hospitals might then be able to build "heart banks" and "liver banks" similar to the blood banks of today. When a heart or liver is needed, doctors could thaw one and use it immediately. Organ banks might also lower the astronomical cost of the major transplant operations.

Transplants using animal organs. In fall of 1984 the California surgeon Dr. Leonard Lee Bailey transplanted a baboon heart into a fourteen-day-old infant called Baby Fae, who was near death because of a heart defect. Baby Fae lived for twenty days but then suddenly died, possibly due to a blood mismatch with the baboon.

Transplanting an organ from one species to another is called *xenografting*. All xenografts of major animal organs into humans have so far failed, including a 1977 operation in which Dr. Christiaan Barnard gave a chimpanzee's heart to a man who lived only three days with it. Nonetheless, xenografting may be a method of the future.

I learned more about xenografting by meeting with Dr. A. Michael Borkon at Johns Hopkins Hospital in Baltimore, Maryland.

Dr. A. Michael Borkon

The young surgeon explained that although pig heart valves and other parts of animal organs help many people, the body tends to reject whole organs from other species much more than it rejects ones from other humans. "The drug cyclosporine helps to combat rejection of an animal organ, but not enough to allow the process to succeed," he said. "I am experimenting with various compounds to see if they help with the rejection problem, but it's too early to tell if they work as yet."

Dr. Borkon made it clear that he is not yet experimenting with animal-human transplants. Instead, he is doing transplants between different species of animals, such as hamsters, rabbits, mice, and rats. If he can find a compound that allows him to do a hamster-rat or hamster-mouse transplant, it might help doctors one day to do transplants between, say, chimpanzees and people.

Dr. Borkon added that animals may provide more than just hearts. "We may be able to use the whole gamut of animal organs— pancreas, kidneys, liver, and so on. We are looking mainly at primates—mainly baboons, apes, and chimps." Dr. Donald Price, a Johns Hopkins expert on Alzheimer's disease, added that doctors are also thinking about grafting brain tissue from animals onto the brains of Alzheimer's disease victims. The animal brain material might help Alzheimer's patients by producing certain substances that their own brains can no longer make.

Dr. Tom Fritz, Dr. A. Michael Borkon, and every other researcher who experiments on animals mentioned something important to them. They dislike seeing animals killed, and they are sorry that this sometimes happens in their experiments. However, they firmly believe that animal experiments are worthwhile because they ultimately save human lives.

Artificial Organs

The Mayo Clinic's Dr. Sylvester Sterioff explained that there probably will never be enough organs from human donors to go around. "At least ten thousand hearts, ten thousand new pancreases, and many thousands of other organs could be used in this country each year," he said. "We'll never have that many human organs available. What will we do about the shortage of human organs? The logical answer is to go to animal organs and artificial organs."

A tremendous amount of research is now being done on artificial organs. When I met with Dr. A. Michael Borkon, he told me that earlier in the day he had placed some artificial hearts in cadavers. He was trying to learn more about what he called the "spatial relationships" of how they fit into the chest.

Artificial hearts, described in Chapter 11, have already achieved some success. In addition, researchers are working to develop other artificial organs, including kidneys and pancreases. In the twenty-first century, the day may come when hospitals will have supply rooms filled with artificial hearts and other mechanical organs. A patient who has a diseased organ may be able to have an artificial one implanted as easily as new parts are now placed in old cars to keep them running. The day could come when artificial organs will be even more durable than the real things!

In Vitro Fertilization

Because of problems with their reproductive systems, some women cannot become pregnant the usual way—by having males release sperm into their vaginas. Until a few years ago, such women could not have their own babies. Then in the late 1970s the *in vitro* fertilization method was developed. This reproductive technique is used mainly for women with missing or damaged oviducts, the tubes in the woman's body where sperm and egg normally unite to produce an embryo. *In vitro* is Latin meaning "in glass." Using this technique, the sperm and the egg are united outside the parents' bodies in a petri dish and then placed in the mother's uterus.

The first successful *in vitro* fertilization was performed in England in November of 1977. A woman with an oviduct disorder had an egg taken from her body. The egg was placed in a petri dish, where it was fertilized by her husband's sperm and began growing into a baby. The embryo was placed back inside the mother's body. On July 25, 1978, the woman gave birth to a daughter she and her husband named Louise. In the years since Louise's birth, several hundred medical centers around the world have begun doing *in vitro* fertilization. The technique has produced more than a thousand children.

To learn about progress with *in vitro* fertilization I met with Dr. G. David Ball of the Mayo Medical School's departments of Obstetrics/Gynecology and Cell Biology. Dr. Ball, who has performed *in vitro* fertilization on more than a thousand eggs, said that improved methods are making the technique increasingly popular.

First of all, doctors have found easier ways of retrieving eggs from a woman. In the "old days" of the late 1970s, a small incision was made in a woman's abdomen to get to her ovaries that contained the eggs. Many women did not want to undergo this operation. In the mid-1980s doctors devised a nonsurgical way of retrieving the eggs. Using ultrasound equipment (devices that locate objects by bouncing high-frequency sound waves off them), doctors spot the ovarian

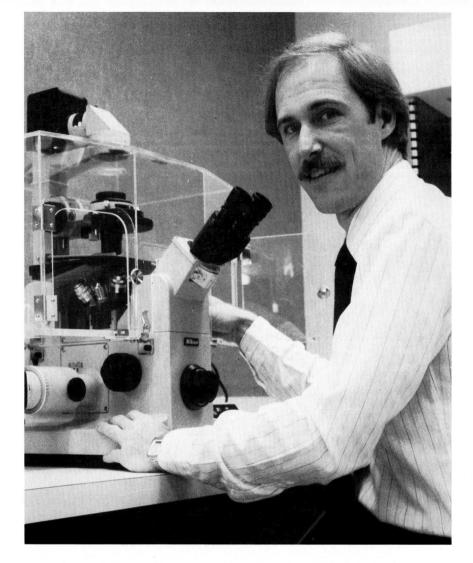

follicles (cavities) that contain the eggs. The doctors then insert an instrument through the woman's vagina and into an ovary, where they retrieve the eggs. Because this method is simpler and less painful than an operation, *in vitro* fertilization is attracting more people than ever before.

Dr. Ball explained that when placed in the woman's uterus, the fertilized egg does not automatically grow into a baby. The health of the embryo, readiness of the woman's uterus to receive the embryo, and other factors determine whether the embryo develops successfully. Because of problems that often occur, pregnancy is established with *in vitro* attempts only about 15 percent of the time.

An experimental method involving freezing of fertilized eggs may improve these numbers. It is not (yet) possible to freeze a human being after birth and later revive him or her. However, it is possible to take an embryo out of the dish where it is growing, freeze it, thaw it several months later, and then place it in its mother's uterus and have it grow. Freezing may improve the chances of a successful pregnancy because it enables doctors to stockpile a large number of the woman's eggs and save them for future attempts at creating a baby. Several frozen embryos have already produced pregnancies, and the technique will probably be used to produce many more.

In vitro fertilization will never be very common, because most women can have children the usual way. Nevertheless, for the thousands who cannot, the improvements of *in vitro* techniques are great news. Showing me a photograph of a fertilized egg in a dish, Dr. Ball added that *in vitro* children have one advantage over those conceived the usual way—much earlier "baby" pictures.

"I can hardly wait until the *in vitro* kids [he helped create] are old enough to see their first baby pictures—taken when they were each just a two-cell embryo."

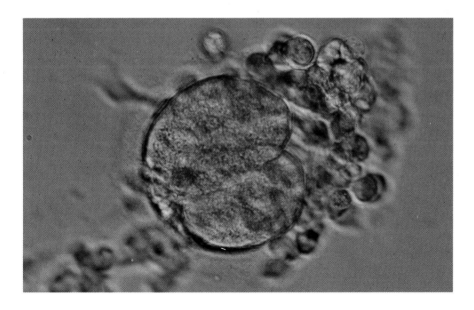

A two-cell human embryo

Chapter 14
Genetic Engineering

If mankind succeeds in improving genetics, genetics may succeed in improving mankind.

Theodosius Dobzhansky, twentieth-century
American biologist

Heredity

Each person, animal, and flower is unique because there will never be another precisely like it. Yet each living thing shares qualities with others of its kind. For example, all elephants are large and all bacteria are tiny compared to people. All starfish can grow new arms when their old ones are broken off, but no person has ever displayed that ability. Furthermore, all mother cats give birth to nothing but kittens and all mother dogs have puppies, while all human mothers have only human babies.

Why is there such regularity within a species? Why has there never been a person who could grow new arms as a starfish does? Why has no mouse grown as big as an elephant, no frog given birth

Gregor Johann Mendel

to a giraffe, and no fish been as intelligent as a chimpanzee? The answer has to do with heredity—the qualities passed down generation after generation to individual living beings. Virtually everything known about heredity has been learned since the 1850s, when the Austrian monk Gregor Johann Mendel (1822–1884) began studying how garden pea plants passed their traits to succeeding generations.

Chromosomes and Genes

The hereditary material of living beings is located in tiny structures in the nuclei (control centers) of all their cells. These tiny structures, which under a powerful microscope sometimes look like Xs, are called *chromosomes*. Each kind of plant and animal has a certain number of chromosomes in each of its body cells. For example, each body cell of a human being has forty-six chromosomes arranged in twenty-three pairs. A gorilla has forty-eight chromosomes in each body cell, a tomato twenty-four, and a giant sequoia tree twenty-two. Chromosomes are so small that fifty thousand human chromosomes laid end to end would reach a length of only one inch!

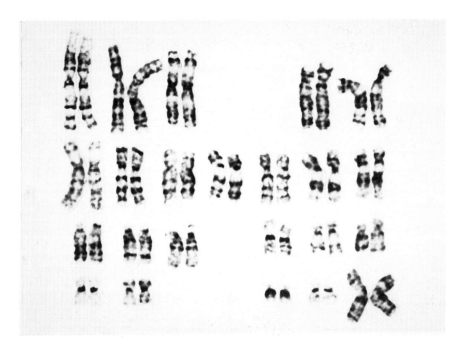

In each human cell there are twenty-three pairs of chromosomes.

183

Chromosomes occur in pairs, except in special cells called *sex cells*. In human males the sex cells are called *sperm*, while in females they are called *eggs*. Each human sperm has twenty-three chromosomes, as does each human egg. When a sperm unites with an egg, the twenty-three chromosomes from the sperm pair up with the twenty-three from the egg, giving the fertilized egg a total of forty-six chromosomes. Each cell of the person who grows from the fertilized egg also has forty-six chromosomes.

A typical chromosome is composed of thousands of units called *genes*, which are the actual units of heredity. If a chromosome is thought of as a kind of bead bracelet, a gene would be somewhat like an individual bead. Genes determine qualities common to an entire species and also ones that distinguish individuals. Most people have genes that ordered their bodies to grow one head, two eyes, and two ears. If not for that, some of us might have three heads, nine eyes, and seventeen ears. Certain genes, though, vary from individual to individual. Among these are genes for height, eye and skin color, intelligence, and personality. Complex qualities such as intelligence are thought to be influenced by dozens of genes.

Almost every cell of an organism's body (not counting the sex cells—egg and sperm) contain all of that individual's genes. A cell from your big toe contains all of your approximately fifty thousand genes, as does a cell from your brain or the tip of your nose. This means that the genes for telling your nose and brain to grow are also located in your feet, intestines, and all other parts of your body. Why don't you grow brains on your elbows or noses in your belly button if brain-growing and nose-growing genes are found in your every cell? The answer is that, in a process not yet understood, genes can be switched on and off, somewhat like lights in a house. While a person's brain is growing to full size, the brain-growing genes are switched on inside the individual's head, but switched off everywhere else. Once the brain reaches full size (at about age six), the brain-growing genes are turned off even inside the head.

Genes are made mainly of deoxyribonucleic acid, usually called

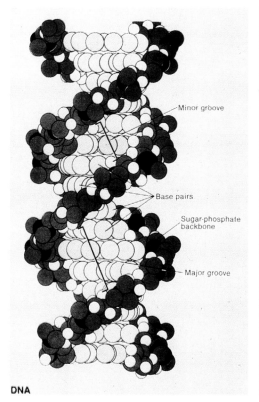

DNA

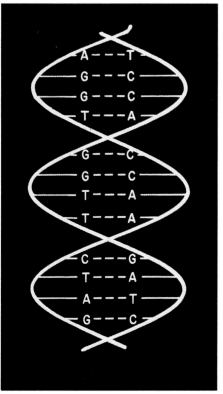

DNA for short. Because it contains the instructions for the development of an organism's traits, DNA is referred to as "the code of life." Complex chemicals that interact with DNA are thought to work the switches that turn genes on and off in certain places at certain times.

The scientific study of genes and heredity is called *genetics,* and the scientists who make these studies are called *geneticists.* Until recent years, most geneticists thought that genes lay beyond human touch, much as the heart and brain were once considered off-limits. Yet just as doctors learned to cure many brain and heart problems earlier in the twentieth century, so they are now unlocking the secrets of genes in the hope of helping people with faulty genes. Manipulating genes for the benefit of people is often called *genetic engineering.* Among the main areas of research in this new field are the production of useful drugs and the cure and prevention of genetic diseases.

Both of the above drawings show the structure of the DNA molecule. A, T, C, and G represent the compounds that form DNA.

185

Producing Drugs with Recombinant DNA Technology

Many people with diabetes cannot produce enough of the hormone insulin on their own, and so sugar accumulates in their blood. Until recently, insulin taken from the pancreases of pigs and cattle was the only source for people in need of the hormone. A problem with this was that there was a limited supply of pig and cattle insulin. Another problem was that people who were allergic to animal insulin could not use it. In the early 1980s a way of making insulin exactly like human insulin was found. Incredibly, scientists used bacteria to make it!

The chemical structure of the human gene responsible for making insulin was determined in 1977. Through a complex process, scientists created an artificial human insulin gene. The synthetic gene was placed into bacteria called *Escherichia coli.*

Like photocopying machines, *E. coli* have the ability to duplicate material. The synthetic insulin-making genes ordered *E. coli* to make insulin! The bacteria obediently produced the hormone. When insulin was made by *E. coli* in 1982, it became the first drug produced through recombinant DNA technology (also called *gene splicing*), a method in which genetic material of different species is combined. Today this genetically engineered insulin is in widespread use among diabetics. There is a limitless supply of this insulin, and it can be taken by those who are allergic to animal insulin.

Recombinant DNA technology has also been used to help children who were not growing properly. Until recently, the only way to obtain a growth hormone for these young people was to harvest it from dead people's pituitary glands. This was expensive—as much as $10,000 a year per patient. Recently doctors have begun using the *E. coli* "drug factories" to reproduce the growth hormone in much the same way that they make insulin.

To learn more about producing drugs with recombinant DNA, I visited Dr. David Fass, a Mayo Medical School cell biology profes-

Molecular biologists working in a recombinant DNA laboratory

sor. Dr. Fass explained that many hemophiliacs (people whose blood does not clot properly) have traditionally been given clotting factors taken from human blood. In the past some patients contracted AIDS or hepatitis from the blood they were given. In 1983 scientists found the human gene for making "factor VIII," the blood clotting substance lacked by most hemophiliacs. They then employed *E. coli* and mammalian cells to help produce factor VIII, which may become available to hemophiliacs in the late 1980s.

Insulin, growth hormone, and factor VIII are among the first triumphs of recombinant DNA technology. In all, at least four thousand genetic diseases (ones caused at least partly by faulty genes) afflict humanity. Many involve the production of the wrong amounts or kinds of substances because genes send faulty messages to the body. In the future, recombinant DNA technology should be useful for producing many substances needed by the victims of genetic diseases.

A crucial step in using bacteria to produce a substance is combining the right human or animal gene or artificial human gene with the bacteria. Unfortunately, scientists have located only a small percentage of the genes that control genetic diseases. However, they are working to identify the genes associated with many other genetic diseases. They do this by making "gene maps."

One way to map genes is to first break apart chromosomes. Each gene on a chromosome contains the blueprint for producing a certain kind of protein (a substance that makes up a large part of each cell). Analysis of the kind of protein it makes reveals a gene's function. As more genes are mapped, scientists will be able to use recombinant DNA technology to treat more genetic diseases.

Gene Therapy

The production of drugs with recombinant DNA technology helps people with genetic defects, but it does not cure them. One day genes may be manipulated to cure or possibly even prevent genetic diseases. *Gene therapy*, as it is called, involves the transplantation of healthy genes into the body. Researchers have already done gene transplants on monkeys and mice, and human gene therapy may be possible in the future.

Here is how gene therapy might work in the year 2050. In that far-off year, people who are in the first stages of a genetic disease enter the hospital for gene transplants. Say, for instance, that the patient's genes cause him or her to develop the serious disorder of the nervous system called Huntington's disease. The patient is given healthy genes that counteract the defective ones.

Where do these healthy genes come from? By this future time, hospitals may have large "libraries" of artificial genes that have been produced by recombinant DNA and other techniques. A hospital technician pulls the good genes that the patient needs off the shelf.

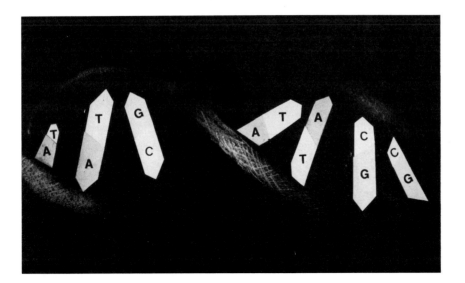

This drawing illustrates DNA base pairing. A pairs with T, and G pairs with C.

Viruses may do the job of getting those healthy genes into the patient's body. It is the nature of viruses to break open and enter cells. Perhaps doctors will take out the harmful contents of viruses, insert the healthy genes into the viruses, and then insert the viruses into the patient. Like dutiful beasts of burden, the viruses carry the healthy genes to the patient's cells, where they counteract the defective genes. Doctors may even develop the ability to remove the patient's defective genes and replace them with the artificial ones.

In the distant future a person who loses an arm, leg, or organ may also be helped by gene therapy, added Dr. Thomas Spelsberg of the Mayo Clinic. Dr. Spelsberg explained that when a baby is growing inside its mother's uterus, genes direct the growth of various body parts. Apparently those genes switch off when a person is fully grown. But doctors may find a way to switch these genes back on, allowing people to grow new limbs and organs.

Major technical problems must be conquered before doctors can transplant genes into people to cure disease. For one thing, scientists have learned the locations of only five hundred of the fifty thousand genes in each human cell and have determined the structure of just a small percentage of those five hundred genes. Before they do gene transplants on people, doctors need to learn more about the location, structure, and function of many more genes. "Also, we need better techniques for delivering the genes to the proper tissue and in the proper position on chromosomes for the genes to function properly," added Dr. Spelsberg. In addition, scientists must learn how to insert the desired gene without risking damage to other genes.

One extremely controversial idea involves gene therapy on the unborn. Scientists may eventually be able to correct genetic defects even before the fetus leaves its mother's uterus.

Say, for instance, that the fetus's genes will make him or her prone to cancer later in life. While the fetus is in the uterus, its defective genes could be replaced with healthy ones. Taking things even further, gene therapy may even be possible *before* a baby is conceived. Dr. Ari Gafni of the University of Michigan's Institute of Gerontology told me that if the genes that control aging are ever found, it may be possible to modify them in the egg and the sperm in order to lengthen people's lives.

Just because scientists develop the ability to do something, it doesn't mean they should do it. There are also ethical problems (questions of right and wrong) to consider. Many people, including some scientists, think that it would be wrong to attempt gene therapy on unborn humans. They say that, no matter how careful scientists might be, mistakes could be made that would damage the unborn. It could also turn out that genes that seem "bad" are necessary for humanity's long-term survival. In addition, many people feel that we do not have the right to "play God" by artificially controlling the traits of future human beings.

Other people, including some geneticists, insist that it is unscientific to rule out the future use of gene therapy on unborn humans. These people think that geneticists should proceed cautiously with animal research (but no research on humans as yet) in this area. They predict that, if all the problems associated with it can be solved, one day gene therapy on unborn humans could be very beneficial.

Chapter 15
A Better and Longer Life
for the Elderly

*You live again, you live again forever; you are young again;
you are young again forever.*

From the end of the ancient
Egyptian "Ritual of Embalming"

*Experience it, as it replenishes youthful fluids. The fluids that
help keep your skin soft, supple, and younger looking. Enjoy it
as it brings out a more youthful radiance, easing away tiny dry
lines, imparting a new suppleness to skin . . . a vibrance that
shows.*

From a skin lotion magazine
advertisement (A.D. 1985)

The Ancient Dream of Longer Life

Healthy people have always wanted to extend their life spans.
One of the world's oldest stories, the Babylonian Epic of Gilgamesh
(2000 B.C. or earlier), describes a hero's quest for immortality. Many
Old Testament heroes were said to have achieved very long lives. For
example, Adam was said to have lived to 930, Noah to 950, and
Methuselah to 969 years of age.

Along with living more years, people have wanted to maintain
their youthfulness. In fact, a long life of increasing feebleness
would be a curse to most people, as the ancient Greek myth of
Tithonus demonstrates. The gods made Tithonus immortal, but ne-
glected to keep him from aging. As a result, Tithonus grew so feeble
that all he could do was sit in a locked room and mindlessly babble
to himself forever.

In real life people have tried some farfetched schemes to try to
prolong their vitality. In ancient Rome some elderly people drank

Gilgamesh holding the herb of immortality

the blood of gladiator fighters who died. They thought the blood of the young contained a vital force that could be transferred to themselves. During the Middle Ages, wealthy people drank mummy dust potions and rubbed mummy powder onto themselves in the hope that the ancient Egyptian methods of preserving the dead could preserve the living. The most famous quest for eternal youth was made by the Spanish explorer Ponce de León, who in 1513 discovered Florida while seeking the Fountain of Youth, a spring that supposedly could make the old young again. Even today some people believe that certain herbs and minerals can impart youthfulness, but no way has ever been found to restore youth to the elderly or keep a person from growing old.

Achieving Our Current Potential

The average life span has climbed over the years—from about age twenty-two in ancient Greece and Rome to about age seventy-five in developed countries today. This increase is due mainly to the conquest of many diseases. However, those ancient people who were not killed by infectious diseases lived to age seventy or more, just as people do today.

As for our potential number of years, that figure probably has not changed much for thousands of years either. Gerontologists (experts on the aging process) think that the longest a person can live today is 125 years. The longest a human being has ever been proved to live is 120½ years. This record is held by Shigechiyo Izumi of Japan, who was born on June 29, 1865, and died on February 21, 1986. The United States longevity record is held by Fanny Thomas, who died at nearly 114 years of age in 1981.

Shigechiyo Izumi of Japan in 1985, when he was 119 years old.

A life of 114 or 120 years is extremely rare. In fact, in the United States only a few thousand people are 100 years of age or older. Although luck and heredity help decide how long each person lives, gerontologists say that people could routinely live to at least 100 by following these rules:

- *Eat moderately to prevent overweight and avoid junk foods and foods high in cholesterol*
- *Get plenty of sleep*
- *Don't smoke*
- *Don't abuse alcohol or drugs*
- *Avoid tension as much as possible*
- *Use caution when crossing streets, driving, and engaging in other hazardous activities*
- *Stay active throughout life*
- *Exercise regularly*
- *Have regular medical checkups and use early cancer detection methods*

People who take care of themselves not only live longer, they also tend to have happier and healthier lives.

Reshaping the Human Life Potential

What about reshaping the human life potential—stretching it to, say, 150 or 200 years? To do that, doctors would have to slow down or halt the aging process. The main reason why doctors cannot do this as yet is that they do not know the causes of aging!

Experiments have shown that human cells do not last forever. When human cells are taken from the body and cultured in a dish, they divide only so many times and then die. Cells from an older person divide a few times before dying. Ones from a newborn baby divide about fifty times before dying. Fifty cell divisions equal about 110 to 120 years. From this, gerontologists conclude that the human life potential is about 120 years, which matches the age achieved by the longest-living people. The question is, why do human cells divide only about fifty times and then die? In other

Dr. David Harrison

words, why do we age and die?

Scientists have numerous theories to explain aging. According to one, we all have "aging genes" that program our cells to last only so long. Another theory asserts that the body's immune system breaks down with age, leading to the steady breakdown of all other systems. A third theory states that over time the brain loses the ability to control production of the proper amounts of vital hormones; too much or too little of the hormones is made, causing organs to break down steadily.

These and other aging theories do not necessarily compete with each other, explained Dr. David Harrison, a research biologist at The Jackson Laboratory in Bar Harbor, Maine. Dr. Harrison said that aging could have several causes, meaning that several theories could be correct. "We simply do not know whether there is one clock [cause] for aging, just a few clocks, or very many clocks."

In his own search for the aging mechanism or mechanisms, Dr. Harrison experiments on mice. So far he has studied ten different

Dr. Ari Gafni

systems in different-aged mice, including immune responses, wound-healing rates, and kidney function. His results so far point to at least a few causes—rather than a single cause—of aging. Other scientists I asked about it—including Dr. Ari Gafni of the University of Michigan's Institute of Gerontology—agreed that aging is probably caused by at least several clocks.

Of course those who dream of stopping the aging process would prefer to find a single cause. Nevertheless, even if aging has many causes, perhaps they could all be controlled by manipulating genes.

"We know that a million years ago the potential human life span was only about 40 years," explained Dr. Ari Gafni, when I visited him at the University of Michigan's Institute of Gerontology in Ann Arbor. "Today it is more than twice that. Probably the change from forty to more than 100 years of potential life involved changes in just a few genes over time. If we could make further changes in those genes, perhaps we could greatly lengthen our potential life span."

Professor Gafni went on to say that the genes might be modified in the sperm and the egg before the individual was conceived. The result might be people who would live far longer than we do today. This cannot occur for many years, because scientists do not yet know where aging genes are located or how to modify them.

There may be simpler ways to lengthen our lives. Instead of turning off the aging switch at the source—the genes—scientists may find ways of interrupting the aging process as it occurs in various human organs.

Dr. Richard C. Adelman, Director of the University of Michigan's Institute of Gerontology, has done important work with a hormone called *somatostatin*, which may help control the aging of at least several organs. When I visited him at the Institute, Dr. Adelman explained that somatostatin exists in virtually every system of the body. "Changes in amount and/or type of somatostatin have been found to accompany the aging of the pancreas, pituitary gland, and brain," said Dr. Adelman, "and it may also be involved in the aging of other systems as well."

Perhaps you are thinking that if doctors returned the amount and/or type of a person's somatostatin to normal levels, aging

Dr. Richard C. Adelman

would be slowed. It is not that simple. "We don't know if differences in somatostatin represent a cause or effect of aging," explained Dr. Adelman. In other words, it is not known whether differences in somatostatin cause organs to age or are a by-product of the aging process.

Other bodily substances have also been linked to aging in unknown ways. Dr. Adelman and other researchers are studying these hormones, enzymes, and other substances that seem to have some connection with aging. Should any of these agents be proven to cause aging, doctors may lead us to the Fountain of Youth by controlling the quality or quantity of these substances in our bodies.

The Mystery of Alzheimer's Disease

People commonly become a bit forgetful when they grow older. For some older people, however, forgetfulness and confusion dominate their lives. Older people suffering from these symptoms are often said to be senile.

Senility has many causes. About 20 percent of the time it is caused by multi-infarct dementia, a disease in which the arteries supplying blood to the brain become clogged. The brain does not receive ample blood, resulting in a series of small strokes that destroy more and more of the brain with time. Another 20 percent of the elderly people labeled "senile" suffer from such problems as brain tumors, thyroid conditions, the overuse of drugs, vitamin deficiencies, poor diet, and mental depression. However, by far the leading cause of senility is Alzheimer's disease, which accounts for about half the cases of senility among the elderly.

Alzheimer's disease (named for German physician Alois Alzheimer, who first identified it in 1906) involves the steady destruction of brain cells. Its symptoms include gradual loss of memory, coordination, and speaking ability, and gradual increase in confusion and often anger. There is no known cure or effective treatment. Its victims eventually cannot care for themselves and generally die of pneumonia or another infection.

Although some Alzheimer's patients are in their forties and fifties, most are over age sixty-five. More than 120,000 of the three million Alzheimer's victims in the United States die of the disease yearly, making it a leading killer of the elderly. These numbers, however, cannot convey the agony Alzheimer's causes families as they watch their loved ones forget names and faces and eventually lose the ability to function.

I met with Dr. Donald Lowell Price, one of the world's foremost Alzheimer's researchers, to see if progress is being made against the disease. In his office at Johns Hopkins Hospital in Baltimore, Maryland, Dr. Price explained that Alzheimer's is difficult to diagnose. Although an autopsy (examination of a dead person) can prove that someone had Alzheimer's, currently the only way to prove that a living person has the disease is to do a brain biopsy (analysis of living tissue). Since it involves surgery, most families do not want their loved ones to undergo biopsies. "That means we must diagnose Alzheimer's by exclusion," said Dr. Price. In other words, if tests show that no other disease is causing the symptoms, doctors think that the patient must have Alzheimer's.

"As for an effective treatment for Alzheimer's disease, so far we have none," continued Dr. Price. "About all we can do is try to help the family."

Adult day-care centers provide companionship and activities for Alzheimer's patients and also help families cope with the disease.

The main reason for this lack of progress is that doctors do not know what causes Alzheimer's disease. "No animal gets Alzheimer's disease, so we can't work with animal models," explained Dr. Price. However, autopsies of Alzheimer's victims have shown that their brains are abnormal in several ways:

- *The nerve cell fibers in the brains of Alzheimer's patients are abnormally twisted*
- *The brains contain plaques—patches of dying nerve fibers that interrupt the flow of information between brain cells*
- *The brains contain unusually large amounts of aluminum*
- *The brains lack the enzyme choline acetyl transferase; this enzyme helps produce the chemical acetylcholine that carries impulses throughout the brain*

Researchers have several theories about the causes of these abnormalities. Some think that "slow viruses" (ones that do no harm for long periods after entering the body) cause Alzheimer's. Since Alzheimer's "runs in" families, it could be a hereditary disease. Possibly harmful chemicals in the environment may cause the disease. As is probably the case with aging in general, Alzheimer's may have more than one cause.

Doctors have tried several experimental treatments on Alzheimer's patients even though they do not yet know the disease's causes. Several drugs have been tried to boost the amount of the impulse-carrying chemical acetylcholine in the brain. So far these drugs have helped Alzheimer's victims only slightly. Doctors are working to develop better drugs and better ways of delivering them to the brain.

"A second idea is grafting," said Dr. Price. Grafting in animals involves taking part of an organ from one living creature and implanting it in another. Cells from normal animal brains would be grafted onto the brains of Alzheimer's patients. The grafted brain cells would produce the acetylcholine and other substances lacked by the patients' brains. This hopefully would help control the disease.

A Better Quality Life for the Elderly

In many developed nations, the elderly have more problems than any other age group. Cancer, heart disease, and Alzheimer's target people in their "golden years." In addition, many of the healthy senior citizens are plagued by poverty, depression, lack of respect from younger people, and low self-esteem.

The good news is that the quality of life among the elderly is improving. One reason for this is that the percentage of elderly people among voters is rising all the time. Between 1900 and 1980 the proportion of Americans sixty-five years old or older rose from about 4 to more than 10 percent. By the year 2030 about 20 percent of the American population will be 65 or older. To get elected and stay in office, lawmakers *must* consider the needs of the elderly.

Dr. Jersey Liang, a research scientist at the University of Michigan's Institute of Gerontology, told me about the need for day-care centers. "Many children of two-career families [ones in which both parents work] are sent to day-care centers," said Dr. Liang. "Those same two-career households cannot care for an elderly parent during the day. The parent often must be placed in a nursing home. It would be better for everyone involved to send these elderly parents to a day-care center. Buses could pick them up in the morning and bring them home later just as is done in some children's day-care centers. Not only would day care be much cheaper than nursing homes, the quality of life would improve for the elderly people because they would be with their families. Everybody wants day-care centers for the elderly. They are the coming thing."

Dr. Liang said that a few privately funded day-care centers for the elderly are already operating. Their clients are mostly wealthier people. The big question is, will the government help pay for day-care centers for the poorer elderly, just as it now pays for day-care centers for children of low-income families? Dr. Liang predicts that in the next few years the public will push the government to support day-care centers for the elderly.

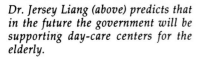

Dr. Jersey Liang (above) predicts that in the future the government will be supporting day-care centers for the elderly.

There is also a need to educate people better about old age, added Dr. Liang. Children are counseled about growing up at school. Movies, books, and other aspects of popular culture also focus on the growing-up years. Yet who is taught to prepare for retirement or the death of a husband or wife—events that cause many older people to fall apart? As more and more of us live long lives, there will probably be more emphasis on preparing for old age.

Dr. Liang concluded by saying that some myths about old age are being laid to rest. "All the textbooks used to say that people in their sixties had a decline in mental and physical fitness. But many of the studies on which those conclusions were based were done on people in nursing homes. We have recently learned that the decline in mental and physical fitness doesn't naturally occur until people are in their late eighties. We have also found that people can be sexually active into their eighties unless there is a problem with illness." Since we now have a good chance of living to at least our eighties, that is good news for everyone!

Chapter 16
Bringing Twentieth-Century Medicine to the Poor

Each year 3.5 million children under age five in the developing world die and another 3.5 million are mentally or physically disabled through six vaccine-preventable diseases: diphtheria, pertussis (whooping cough), tetanus, measles, polio, and tuberculosis. Only about 25 percent of the 100 million children born into the developing world each year are currently vaccinated against all or most of these diseases.

Information from UNICEF's 1987 report,
The State of the World's Children

Even when there is no special famine going on, over 14 million of the world's children under age five die annually as a result of the combination of malnutrition and disease.

Kristina Schellinski,
UNICEF information officer

Although medicine has a very promising future, we must remember that millions of the world's people might as well be living in the year 1800 as far as their medical care is concerned. These people live in the poorest nations. For them, new medical breakthroughs have little meaning. What they need is the basic medical care that most people in the wealthier countries take for granted.

Now and then a famine (prolonged food shortage), such as the one that occurred in Ethiopia and other African nations during the 1980s, makes the headlines. Few people, however, realize that hunger is a way of life for many millions of the world's people, even when no widespread famine is occurring. About 30 percent of our fellow human beings, or about 1½ billion people, are thought to be malnourished almost all of the time.

Hunger has a deadly companion: disease. People weakened by hunger lack the strength to fight off disease. These people also usu-

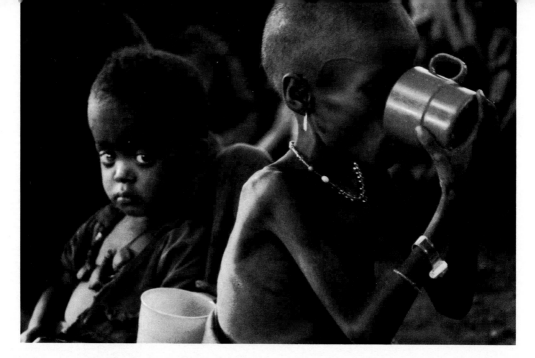

Victims of the devastating drought in Ethiopia suffer the effects of malnutrition.

ally lack the money for good medical care. Many of them have not received the immunizations that are routinely given to children in the wealthier nations. Weakened by hunger and unprotected by immunizations, they fall victim to a variety of diseases including influenza, diarrhea, typhus, measles, diphtheria, whooping cough, tetanus, tuberculosis, and polio.

Children and the elderly are the prime targets of the malnutrition-disease combination. How many million elderly people in the poor nations die each year of this deadly combination is unknown. But the United Nations Children's Emergency Fund (UNICEF) estimates that malnutrition and disease kill more than 14 million children yearly even when no large-scale famine is occurring.

It is difficult to comprehend what *14 million* dead children per year means. The number is roughly equal to all the people in New York City, Chicago, Los Angeles, and Boston added together.

The most tragic aspect of these deaths is that nearly all of them could be prevented, explained Kristina Schellinski, a UNICEF information officer. It costs just a few dollars to immunize a child against six common and dangerous diseases: measles, whooping cough, tetanus, polio, tuberculosis, and diphtheria. Despite that low cost, only 25 percent of the children in the poorest nations receive these

Above: UNICEF information officer Kristina Schellinski. Right: A child being immunized

immunizations. Reasons for this include lack of money, medical supplies, and personnel to administer the immunizations.

Working with the governments of the poorer nations, UNICEF and several other relief organizations are providing immunizations for millions of children against the six diseases just mentioned. "UNICEF's goal is to immunize virtually every last child in the world against these diseases by 1990," said Kristina Schellinski. Even if this could be done by the year 2000, it would be one of the greatest lifesaving achievements in the history of medicine.

"Oral rehydration therapy" is another lifesaving project being undertaken by UNICEF and several other relief organizations. It involves passing out inexpensive packets of salt, sugar, and a little potassium to millions of children in nearly one hundred nations. The purpose of these packets (the contents of which are to be mixed with water) is to save the children from dehydration (loss of water) caused by diarrhea, an affliction that claims the lives of 3.5 million children yearly and is the biggest single killer of the very young.

At the end of 1986 UNICEF reported some good news concerning immunization and oral rehydration therapy. During the year 1986 these two simple measures had saved the lives of more than 1½ million children worldwide. However, the goals of widespread immunization and oral rehydration therapy are far from met. Approximately 3.5 million children died in 1986 because of dehydration from diarrhea, and about the same number died of diseases that are vaccine-preventable.

Hunger, too, is being battled by many organizations, including UNICEF, the Red Cross, Oxfam, CARE, Save the Children, and World Relief. Relief organizations don't just bring in food. They help the people of poorer nations build irrigation projects so that water can be brought to their crops. They teach them about improved seeds that will yield more bountiful crops. They also show farmers how to conserve their precious soil. Teaching people to produce more food for themselves is a more permanent solution to the hunger problem than just bringing in food for them.

Overpopulation is another problem in many poor countries. Between 1900 and 1987 the world's population more than tripled, growing from about 1.5 billion to nearly 5 billion people. Most of this growth occurred in the poorer nations, placing a burden on their already meager food supplies. Recently the governments and medical personnel of many poorer nations have encouraged their people to plan smaller families. These efforts are starting to pay off. In the mid-1980s, the global population growth began to slow for the first time ever.

As new cancer treatments and artificial organs make headlines in future years, we must remember that basic medical care is still lacking for millions of poor people. Can medicine ever be called successful while so many people are living short, unhappy lives because of a lack of basic medical care?

Glossary

acupuncture—a Chinese method of puncturing the body with needles at various points to treat disease or relieve pain or provide anesthesia for surgery

AIDS (Acquired Immune Deficiency Syndrome)—a condition caused by a virus in which the body's natural defense system against infections is damaged, allowing diseases that are normally fought off by the body to become deadly

alveoli—tiny air sacs in the lungs where oxygen and the waste carbon dioxide are exchanged

anatomy—the structure of living beings

anemia—a condition in which there is a reduction in the number of red blood cells or of the coloring material (hemoglobin) that carries oxygen in the blood

anesthetic—a substance that prevents feeling, especially pain

aneurysm—a weakened portion of the wall of a blood vessel that may balloon outward

antibiotic—a drug that fights or kills infecting germs such as bacteria

antibody—an infection-fighting substance produced within the body; it reacts with an antigen

antigen—a substance that can stimulate the immune system to defend the body

antiseptic—a germ-killing substance

aseptic—free from germs

atrium—an upper chamber of the heart

autopsy—examination of a dead body to determine cause of death or the effects of disease

bacterium—a microscopic germ that causes disease

biopsy—an examination of living tissue removed from the body

bronchoscope—an instrument used for studying the inside of bronchial tubes (breathing passages)

bronchus—an air passage to the lungs

cadaver—a dead body

carcinogen—a cancer-causing substance

catheter—a small tube that can be inserted into body openings to inject or withdraw fluids

cesarean section—the delivery of a baby through an incision in the mother's abdomen and uterus

chemotherapy—the use of drugs to combat disease

chromosomes—threadlike coils within the core of every living cell that contain the genetic program of the entire person

communicable disease—a disease that can be passed from person to person

cornea—the transparent outer covering of the eyeball

cystoscope—an instrument used for studying the inside of the bladder

depression—a condition of prolonged sadness

electrocardiograph—an instrument used for recording the electrical activity of the heart (heartbeat)

embryo—a fertilized egg up to two months after fertilization

endocrine gland—a cellular structure that discharges substances called hormones directly into the bloodstream

enzyme—a substance that speeds up chemical processes in the body

epidemic—a large-scale outbreak of a disease within a community or area

epidemiologist—a medical specialist who studies the occurrence of disease among large numbers of people

exocrine gland—a cellular structure that releases substances into the intestines or to the outside of the body

fertilization—the uniting of an egg and a sperm to begin the development of a new person

fetus—an unborn baby more than two months past fertilization

gene—the unit of heredity found in chromosomes that determines traits and characteristics

genetics—the scientific study of genes and heredity

heredity—the qualities and characteristics passed down generation after generation to individual living beings

hormone—a chemical messenger secreted by an endocrine gland directly into the bloodstream that carries it to various parts of the body where it directs cell activity

hygiene—cleanliness

hypertension—a higher than normal pressure of the blood pushing against the artery wall as the blood moves from the heart through the body; also called high blood pressure

hypodermic syringe—a device used for injecting substances into or beneath the skin

immunity—the ability of the body to fight off a particular disease

incision—a surgical opening into the body

insulin—the hormone that regulates the body's use of sugar

larynx—the voice box

malnutrition—a general lack of nourishing food

marrow—the tissue inside the bone cavities where blood cells are made

metabolism—the rate at which food and oxygen are used by the body

metastasis—the spread of cancer from the first site where it appears to new sites

microbe—a microscopic organism that causes disease

monoclonal antibodies—special identical proteins that have the ability to seek out foreign substances

nerve—a bundle of nerve cells; neurons

neuron—a nerve cell

obstetrics—the branch of medicine that deals with pregnancy and childbirth

oncogenes—normal genes that upon stimulation cause uncontrolled cell division (cancer) to develop

open-heart surgery—a surgical procedure in which the chest is opened so that the heart can be operated on

ophthalmology—the branch of medicine that deals with the structure and diseases of the eye

ophthalmoscope—an instrument for studying the inside of the eye

organ transplant—a surgical procedure in which a failing organ is replaced with a working organ taken from either a living or dead person

pasteurization—a process by which germs in a substance are killed by heat without changing the substance

pharynx—the area behind the tongue that combines the nasal passages and the throat

phobia—a strong fear of a certain object or situation

psychiatry—the branch of medicine that deals with mental disorders

psychotherapy—a treatment method in psychiatry in which the patient talks about his or her mental problems in order to understand them better

public health—the branch of medicine that deals with the protection and improvement of the health of a community

rabies—a disease caused by a virus that attacks cells in the nervous system

radiology—the branch of medicine that deals with the use of X rays in the diagnosis and treatment of disease

retina—the lining of the eye that receives the image that is being seen

saliva—the secretion from the salivary glands in the mouth that moistens and begins digesting food

stethoscope—an instrument consisting of earpieces, hollow tubing, and a contact piece that picks up sounds from a person's heart, lungs, and blood vessels

thrombus—a blood clot that is formed within a blood vessel

transfusion—a transfer of blood from a container outside the body into the vein of a person

vaccination—a process by which dead or harmless germs of a disease are introduced into the body in order to stimulate the body to produce disease-fighting substances against that illness

venereal disease—a disease transmitted by sexual contact

ventricle—a lower chamber of the heart

virus—a germ that causes disease

vitamins—substances that are present in food and are necessary for good nutrition

X ray—a form of energy that can penetrate solid substances and reveal what is inside

Bibliography

History of Medicine

Bedeschi, Giulio — *Science of Medicine*. F. Watts, New York. 1975.

Bowen, Robert Sidney — *They Found the Unknown: The Stories of Nine Great Discoveries in the Field of Medical Knowledge*. Macrae Smith, Philadelphia. 1963.

Cohen, Daniel — *The Last 100 Years, Medicine*. M. Evans, New York. 1981.

Crook, Bette Jean — *Famous Firsts in Medicine*. Putnam, New York. 1974.

Eberle, Irmengarde — *Modern Medical Discoveries*. Crowell, New York. 1968.

Eldon, Kathy — *The Story of Medicine*. Wayland, Hove, England. 1977.

Fekete, Irene — *Diseases and Medicine*. Facts on File, New York. 1985.

Hudson, Robert P. — *Disease and Its Control: The Shaping of Modern Thought*. Greenwood Press, Westport, Conn. 1983.

Hume, Ruth — *Great Men of Medicine*. Random House, New York. 1961.

Hume, Ruth — *Great Women of Medicine*. Random House, New York. 1964.

Kalman, Bobbie — *Early Health & Medicine*. Crabtree Pub. Co., New York. 1983.

Lee, Russel V. — *The Physician*. Time, New York. 1967.

Lehrer, Steven — *Explorers of the Body*. Doubleday, Garden City, New York. 1979.

Lyons, Albert S. — *Medicine: An Illustrated History*. Abrams, New York. 1978.

Nuland, Sherwin — *Doctors: The Biography of Medicine*. Knopf, New York. 1988.

Robbin, Irving — *Giants of Medicine*. Grosset and Dunlap, New York. 1962.

Robinson, Donald B. — *The Miracle Finders: The Stories Behind the Most Important Breakthroughs of Modern Medicine*. McKay, New York. 1976.

Rosenberg, Lawrence — *The Story of Modern Medicine*. Norton, New York. 1966.

Shippen, Katherine — *Men of Medicine*. Viking Press, New York. 1957.

Stevens, Gareth — *Famous Names in Medicine*. Wayland, Hove, England. 1979.

Trotter, Wilfred — *Man the Healer*. Priory Press, London. 1975.

Weissmann, Gerald — *They All Laughed at Christopher Columbus: Tales of Medicine and the Art of Discovery*. Times Books, New York. 1987.

Human Anatomy

Allison, Linda — *Blood and Guts: A Working Guide to Your Own Insides*. Little, Brown, Boston. 1976.

Bruun, Ruth — *The Human Body*. Random House, New York. 1982.

Caselli, Giovanni — *The Human Body and How It Works*. Grosset & Dunlap, New York. 1987.

Daly, Kathleen N. — *Body Words: A Dictionary of the Human Body, How It Works, and Some of the Things that Effect It*. Warwick Press, New York. 1980.

Elting, Mary — *The Macmillan Book of the Human Body*. Aladdin Books, New York. 1986.

Fekete, Irene — *Your Body*. Facts on File, New York. 1984.

Gabb, Michael — *Secrets of the Human Body*. R. Rourke Pub. Co., Windermere, Fla. 1980.

Knight, Bernard	*Discovering the Human Body: How Pioneers of Medicine Solved the Mysteries of the Body's Structure and Function.* Lippincott & Crowell, New York. 1980.
Kramer, Ann (ed.)	*The Human Body.* World Book, Chicago. 1986.
National Geographic	*The Incredible Machine.* National Geographic Society, Washington, D.C. 1986.
National Geographic	*Your Wonderful Body.* National Geographic Society, Washington, D.C. 1982.
Nourse, Alan Edward	*The Body.* Time-Life Books, Alexandria, Va. 1980.
Packard, Mary	*From Head to Toe: How Your Body Works.* Julian Messner, New York. 1985.
Rand McNally	*Rand McNally Atlas of the Human Body.* Rand McNally, New York. 1976.
Reader's Digest	*ABC's of the Human Body.* Reader's Digest Assoc., Pleasantville, New York. 1987.
Rutland, Jonathan	*Human Body.* Warwick Press, New York. 1976.
Vannini, Vanio (editor).	*The Color Atlas of Human Anatomy.* Harmony Books, New York. 1980.
Walpole, Brenda	*Simon & Schuster's Pocket Book of the Human Body.* Simon & Schuster, New York. 1986.
Ward, Brian R.	*Body Maintenance.* Franklin Watts, New York. 1983.
Wilson, Ron	*How the Body Works.* Larousse, New York. 1978.
Wong, Ovid K.	*Your Body and How It Works.* Childrens Press, Chicago. 1986.

Disease and Illness

Anderson, Madelyn Klein	*Environmental Diseases.* F. Watts, New York. 1987.
Arnold, Caroline	*Pain: What Is It? How Do We Deal with It?* Morrow, New York. 1986.
Berger, Melvin	*Disease Detectives.* Crowell, New York. 1978.
Bershad, Carol	*Bodyworks: The Kids' Guide to Food and Physical Fitness.* Random House, New York. 1979.
Brown, Fern G.	*Hereditary Diseases.* F. Watts, New York. 1987.
Eagles, Douglas A.	*Nutritional Diseases.* F. Watts, F. 1987.
Fekete, Irene	*Disease and Medicine.* Facts on File, New York. 1985.
Goldsmith, Ilse	*Why You Get Sick and How You Get Well.* Sterling Pub., New York. 1970.
Knight, David C.	*Viruses, Life's Smallest Enemies.* W. Morrow, New York. 1981.
Landau, Elaine	*Alzheimer's Disease.* F. Watts, New York. 1987.
Metos, Thomas H.	*Communicable Disease.* F. Watts, New York. 1987.
Nourse, Alan Edward	*Viruses.* F. Watts, New York. 1983.
Riedman, Sarah Regal	*Diabetes.* F. Watts, New York. 1980.
Settel, Joanne	*Why Does My Nose Run? (And Other Questions Kids Ask About Their Bodies).* Atheneum, New York. 1985.
Stedman, Nancy	*The Common Cold and Influenza.* Messner, New York. 1986.
Stiller, Richard	*Your Body Is Trying to Tell You Something: How to Understand and Respond to Its Needs.* Harcourt Brace Jovanovich, New York. 1979.
Tiger, Steven	*Arthritis.* Messner, New York. 1986.
Tiger, Steven	*Diabetes.* Messner, New York. 1987.

Heart Disease

Davis, Goode P.	*The Heart, The Living Pump*. U.S. News Books, Washington, D.C. 1981.
Dunbar, Robert E.	*The Heart and the Circulatory System*. F. Watts, New York. 1984.
Page, Jake	*Blood, The River of Life*. U.S. News Books, Washington, D.C. 1981.
Gaskin, John	*The Heart*. F. Watts, New York. 1985.
McGowen, Tom	*The Circulatory System: From Harvey to the Artificial Heart*. F. Watts, New York. 1988.
Silverstein, Alvin	*Heart Disease: America's #1 Killer*. Lippincott, New York. 1985.
Silverstein, Alvin	*Heartbeats*. Lippincott, New York. 1983.
Tiger, Steven	*Heart Disease*. J. Messner, New York. 1986.
Ward, Brian R.	*The Heart and Blood*. F. Watts, New York. 1982.

Cancer

Berger, Melvin	*Cancer Lab*. John Day Co., New York. 1975.
Burns, Sheila	*Cancer, Understanding and Fighting It*. J. Messner, New York. 1982.
Fine, Judylaine	*Afraid to Ask: A Book About Cancer*. Lothrop, Lee & Shepard Books, New York. 1986.
Fradin, Dennis	*Cancer*. Childrens Press, Chicago. 1988.
Gravelle, Karen	*Teenagers Face-to-face with Cancer*. J. Messner, New York. 1986.
Haines, Gail Kay	*Cancer*. F. Watts, New York. 1980.
Hyde, Margaret O.	*Cancer in the Young: A Sense of Hope*. Westminster Press, Philadelphia. 1985.
Silverstein, Alvin	*Cancer: Can It be Stopped*. Lippincott, New York. 1987.
Trull, Patti	*On with My Life*. Putnam, New York. 1983.

Medicine Today and Tomorrow

Ardley, Neil	*Health and Medicine*. F. Watts, New York. 1982.
Aylesworth, Thomas G.	*The Search for Life*. Rand McNally, Chicago. 1975.
Cross, Wilbur	*The New Age of Medical Discovery*. Hawthorn, New York. 1972.
Durie, Bruce	*Medicine*. Silver Burdett Press, Morristown, N.J. 1988.
Holmes, Fiona	*Medicine*. British Broadcasting Corp., London. 1985.
Jackson, Gordon	*Medicine*. F. Watts, New York. 1984.
Jacobs, Francine	*Breakthrough: The True Story of Penicillin*. Dodd, Mead, New York. 1985.
Kettelkamp, Larry	*The Healing Arts*. Morrow, New York. 1978.
Lambert, Mark	*Medicine in the Future*. Bookwright Press, New York. 1986.
Lee, Essie E.	*A Matter of Life and Technology: Health Sciences Today*. Messner, New York. 1986.
McAleer, Neil	*The Body Almanac: Mind Boggling Facts About Today's Human Body and High Tech Medicine*. Doubleday, Garden City, New York. 1985.
Rosen, Stephen	*Future Facts: A Forecast of the World as We Will Know It Before the End of the Century*. Simon and Schuster, New York. 1978.
Stwertka, Eve	*Computers in Medicine*. F. Watts, New York. 1984.
Toure, Halima	*Pain*. Watt, New York. 1981.

Tully, Marianne	*Dread Diseases.* F. Watts, New York. 1978.
Wickham, Nicholas	*Medical Technology.* F. Watts, New York. 1986.
Winn, Marie	*The Sick Book: Questions and Answers About Hiccups and Mumps, Sneezes and Bumps and Other Things that Go Wrong with Us.* Four Winds Press, New York. 1976.
Zim, Herbert Spencer	*Medicine.* Morrow, New York. 1974.

Transplants, Bionics, and *In Vitro* Fertilization

Bender, David	*Science and Religion: Opposing Viewpoints.* Greenhaven Press, St. Paul, Minn. 1985.
Cauwels, Janice M.	*The Body Shop: Bionic Revolutions in Medicine.* Mosby, St. Louis. 1986.
Dolan, Edward	*Matters of Life and Death.* F. Watts, New York. 1982.
Freese, Arthur S.	*The Bionic People Are Here.* McGraw-Hill, New York. 1978.
Leinwand, Gerald	*Transplants: Today's Medical Miracles.* Watts, New York. 1985.
Madison, Arnold	*Transplanted and Artificial Body Organs.* Beaufort Books, New York. 1981.
Metos, Thomas H.	*Artificial Humans: Transplants and Bionics.* J. Messner, New York. 1985.
Skurzynski, Gloria	*Bionic Parts for People: The Real Story of Artificial Organs and Replacement Parts.* Four Winds Press, New York. 1978.
Snyder, Gerald	*Test-tube Life: Scientific Advance and Moral Dilemma.* J. Messner, New York. 1982.

Human Genetics

Arnold, Caroline	*Genetics: From Mendel to Gene Splicing.* F. Watts, New York. 1986.
Asimov, Isaac	*How Did We Find Out About Genes?* Walker, New York. 1983.
Bornstein, Sandy	*New Frontiers in Genetics.* J. Messner, New York. 1984.
Facklam, Margery	*From Cell to Clone: The Story of Genetic Engineering.* Harcourt Brace Jovanovich, New York. 1979.
Gutnik, Martin J.	*Genetics.* F. Watts, New York. 1985.
Oleksy, Walter C.	*Miracles of Genetics.* Childrens Press, Chicago. 1986.
Silverstein, Alvin	*The Genetics Explosion.* Four Winds Press, New York. 1980.
Snyder, Gerald S.	*Test-tube Life: Scientific Advance and Moral Dilemma.* J. Messner, New York. 1982.
Stwertka, Eve	*Genetic Engineering.* F. Watts, New York. 1982.

Index

germ theory, 10, 44–47, 95, 97
gerontologists, 193
gigantism, 90
Gilchrist, Gerald, 143
Gill, William, 139
glands, 89–91, 105
glycogen, 91
Golden Mirrors of Medicine, 12
gonorrhea, 95
Gordon, Alexander, 46
gout, 102–103, 164
grafting, 200
Greece, medicine in ancient, 15–18
Greenberg, Alan, 157
Grimm, Richard H., Jr., 147
growth hormone, 187
Gutenburg, Johannes, 26
gynecologists, 112

H

Harrison, David, 195–196
Harvey, William, 12, 32–33
heart, 79, 81–82
heart attacks, 98
    preventing, 145–146
heart disease, 201
heart-lung machine, 65, 115
heart transplant, 66, 150, 172
heart valve operations, 123
Helmholtz, Hermann von, 53
hematologists, 113
hemoccult tests, 138
hepatitis, 117–118
heredity, 182–183
hernias, 123
Herodotus, 16
heroin, 119
Hinshaw, David, 172
Hippocrates, 16–18, 94
"Hippocratic Collection," 17
Hippocratic Oath, 10, 16
HIV (human immunodeficiency virus), 168
Holmes, Oliver Wendell, 46
Hopkins, Sir Frederick Gowland, 56
hormonal diseases, 103–105
hormones, 89, 90, 91, 103
hospitals, 115–117
    in ancient Rome, 18
Huang-ti, 12
Humana Heart Institute, 152
human immunodeficiency virus (HIV), 168
human life potential, reshaping, 194–198
hunger, 203, 206
Hunter, John, 36
Huntington's disease, 188
hygiene, and disease prevention, 44–45, 47

electron microscopes, 58, 94
embryo, 93
emphysema, 103
endocrine glands, 89, 103
endocrinologists, 112
enoximone, 155
enzymes, 86
epiglottis, 86
epidemics, 14
    causes of, 14–15, 18, 21
    prevention of, 14
epidemiologists, 112
epiglottis, 86
erythrocytes, 79–80
esophagus, 86
ether, 41, 43
ether frolics, 41
Euripides, 16
Exercitatio Anatomica de Motu Cordis et Sanguinis in Animalibus (An Anatomical Treatise on the Motion of the Heart and Blood in Animals) (Harvey), 33
exocrine glands, 90
eyes, 74–75

F

factor VIII, 187
famine, 203
Fass, David, 186–187
feces, 87
fetus, 93
fish oil, 146
Fleming, Alexander, 60–61
foxglove, 36
fracture, 109
Freud, Sigmund, 63
Fritz, Tom, 132, 178
fungi, 94
Funk, Casimir, 56

G

Gafni, Ari, 190, 196–197
Galen, 18–19, 23, 27–28
Galileo, 32
gastroenterologists, 112
general surgeons, 112
genes, 183–185
gene splicing, 186
gene therapy, 188–190
genetic engineering, 182, 185
    and chromosomes, 183–185
    and genes, 183–185, 188–190
    heredity, 182–183
    recombinant DNA technology, 186–188
geneticists, 185
genetics, 185
German measles, 117, 118
germs, 95

tonsillectomy, 123
tonsillitis, 123
trachea, 84
tranquilizers, 119
transplants, 66–67, 124–125, 162–163, 172–178
trephination, 11
tuberculosis, 64, 118, 204
typhus, 204

U

V

W

X

Y

Z

Photo Credits

About the Author

Dennis Fradin is the author of nearly one hundred children's books. His previous books for Childrens Press include the DISASTER! series and the YOUNG PEOPLE'S STORIES OF OUR STATES. His recent works include a science-fiction novel entitled *How I Saved The World*, published by Dillion Press; a nonfiction book about remarkable children published by Little, Brown; and *Medicine* published by Childrens Press. He has also written stories and articles for many magazines including *The Saturday Evening Post, Scholastic, National Humane Review,* and *Illinois Issues.* Married and the father of two sons and a daughter, Dennis enjoys playing baseball in his free time.